Models of Defaults

A self-contained overview of the main default models used in the Finance industry

Fabien Mercier

Editeur : CSIPP
ISBN-13 : 978-1535321143
ISBN-10 : 1535321148

© 2016 Fabien Mercier. Tous droits réservés.

Contents

1 **Executive summary**   3

2 **Introduction and motivation**   5
   2.1 Credit claims and Asset-Backed Securities in the European context 5
   2.2 Scope of the book 6
   2.3 Detailed outline of the structure of the book 7
   2.4 Notation and preliminaries 9
      2.4.1 Random variables for modelling default 9
      2.4.2 Granularity of a portfolio and Herfindahl index 12
      2.4.3 Definitions of defaults 13

3 **Description of main default models**   15
   3.1 Structural models 15
      3.1.1 The Merton model 15
      3.1.2 The Vasicek one-factor model for pools 19
      3.1.3 The Gordy/Vasicek model and Basel II capital requirements 21
   3.2 Statistical models 23
      3.2.1 The copula approach 23
      3.2.2 Lévy process approach 27

4 **Alternative default models**   31
   4.1 Hidden markov chain models 31
      4.1.1 Motivation 31
      4.1.2 Description of the two-states binomial HMM and implementation 32
      4.1.3 European speculative grade corporate defaults 34
      4.1.4 European pool data from Bloomberg 38
   4.2 Cox-modelling of default rates 43

		4.2.1 Motivation	43

- 4.2.1 Motivation 43
- 4.2.2 Survival analysis modelling of the hazard rate 46
- 4.2.3 Modelling choices 47
- 4.2.4 Final model 52
- 4.2.5 Model interpretation and consequences for risk assessment 53

5 Conclusion 55

6 Annex 1: formal proofs, derivations 61
- 6.1 Proof of the intensity model formula when $PD_i(t)$ is derivable 61
- 6.2 Merton threshold derivation 62
- 6.3 CreditMetrics as a Merton model of default 62
- 6.4 From Merton to Vasicek 63
- 6.5 Vasicek derivation of pool default rate distribution for large homogenous portfolios 64
- 6.6 VaR and ES in Gordy and Vasicek framework 65
- 6.7 Simulating the reduced Gaussian copula model 67

7 Annex 2: Hidden Markov Chains 69
- 7.1 Efficient algorithms 69
  - 7.1.1 Expressing the likelihood 69
  - 7.1.2 The first step 71
  - 7.1.3 Obtention of confidence interval through parametric bootstrap 74
  - 7.1.4 Obtention of h step forward forecasts from the model . 74
  - 7.1.5 Assessing the goodness-of-fit of the model through the forward mid-pseudo residuals 75
  - 7.1.6 Non-homogeneous hidden Markov chains 76
  - 7.1.7 An example with binomially-simulated data 77

Abstract

This book is concerned with the modelling of defaults. It explains the most widely used default models in a self-contained way, with consistent notations across models, while indicating links between models and each model use and limitations. It also presents two innovative ways to model defaults, with an application in a European context. The first model uses hidden Markov chains to estimate the (unobservable) state of the credit cycle, and the resulting default rates, without making any assumptions on the main drivers of the credit cycle. The second model is derived from Survival Analysis, and uses Cox-models and loan-level data retrieved from the European DataWarehouse to uncover the relative riskiness of credit claims backing eligible SME ABS. It allows to extract from the loan-level data a precise multivariate relative-risk assessment of each individual loan on the basis of its characteristics, as recorded in the 138 fields currently available in the SME ABS loan-level data template. It thus represents a very useful complementary model for any risk-modeller wanting to take advantage of this massive database in its credit assessment.

Keywords: credit risk; default risk modelling; pools of credit claims; hidden Markov chains; Survival Analysis; Cox model; credit cycle

JEL classification: C13, G15, G17, G32

Chapter 1

Executive summary

This book focuses on the estimation and modelling of defaults, both for firms and for specific types of loans and debt instruments.
It provides a comprehensive overview of the default models most widely used in finance and risk management in a self-contained way, with consistent notations across the various models, revealing the links between models as well as each model's use, limitations and extensions.
The book also presents two new and less well-known promising types of models for estimating and predicting defaults. The two models are tested in this book using data on the performance of Spanish small and medium sized (SME) loans in Asset Backed Securities (ABS), in particular loan-level data stored in the European Data Warehouse.
The first type of innovative model borrows techniques from the speech recognition literature to estimate the credit cycle of a particular sector of the economy based on a time series of realised defaults. Our results confirm that most sectors go through "credit cycles", which can be distinct from business cycles and estimated independently from traditional macro-economic variables if long-enough time series of realised defaults are available. Within each phase of the cycle (low default risk / high default risk), the model is able to efficiently estimate different probability of defaults for loans belonging to that sector, using data from Bloomberg. The required efficient algorithms are provided in an annex and are crucial to the implementation of the model, as direct computation is not achievable.
The second type of innovative model borrows techniques from survival analysis literature to allow for more granular default probability estimations, using loan-level data from Spanish SME ABS transactions. Our model uses rigorous statistical methods traditionally used in medicine, but largely unknown in finance, to produce loan-specific relative risk assessments, leveraging the

very large data set to achieve granular estimations. We estimated risk scores that quantify each characteristic of an individual loan in terms of how much it increases the probability of default, holding all other characteristics, as well as some selected macro-economic variables, constant. Of all the loan characteristics that were tested, we find that the loan purpose is the most relevant for the risk of default, with "debt-consolidation" increasing twofold the rate of default compared to loans whose purpose was for investment, i.e. "purchase of equipment". The legal form, the borrower's Basel 3 segment, the type of collateral used, as well as the initial interest spread charged to the borrower at origination of the loan, are also crucial explanatory variables in Spanish SME loan riskiness, with the impact on the default rate being of a similar magnitude than a 1% variation of the Gross-Domestic Product (GDP).

Chapter 2

Introduction and motivation

2.1 Credit claims and Asset-Backed Securities in the European context

The Eurosystem is currently accepting both **individual credit claims and pools of credit claims** as collateral for its monetary operations. Individual credit claims have always been accepted in the general collateral framework. In December 2011, the Governing Council decided to allow National Central Banks (NCBs) to temporarily extend eligibility to other performing credit claims based on NCB-specific eligibility and risk control frameworks, albeit on a non-loss-sharing basis. The credit claims eligible on the basis of such specific frameworks are referred to as the Additional Credit Claims (ACC). They can be pledged as individual credit claims or as whole pools of credit claims.[1] These pools can contain credit claims with a higher probability of default than the individual credit claims which are eligible as collateral through the general collateral framework. This is because diversification effects are taken into account at the pool level through the use of a model for default rates in pools of assets. These NCB-specific frameworks are still subject to minimum risk-control requirements, in the sense that the Governing Council has set minimum eligibility criteria for credit claims to be accepted. As of end of Q3 2014, the resulting aggregate value of credit claims after haircuts pledged to the Eurosystem (both through the general framework and through the ACC

---

[1]The Governing Council approved ACC frameworks, including their associated haircuts. Hence, the three main features of ACC frameworks are that (1) they operate under a *non-risk sharing regime*, meaning that the potential losses in a given ACC framework will solely be borne by its NCB, (2) they were conceived as a *temporary measure* to expand collateral availability in the Eurosystem, and (3) entire pools of credit claims can be pledged.

frameworks) was 362 billion[2]. This is an amount similar to the total amount of government securities pledged, and about 19% of the total amount of liquidity provided to the Eurosystem.

Credit claims also make up the pools backing **Asset-Backed Securities (ABS)**, which is another asset class accepted as collateral by the Eurosystem. ABS are financial instruments made bankruptcy remote from their originator. In case of originator default, investors are directly exposed to the default risk of the credit claims that form the ABS pool, as the cash-flows they become entitled to are generated from the credit claims of the pool. As of end of Q3 2014, 306.2 billion of ABSs were pledged to the Eurosystem, which represents about 17% of the total amount of liquidity provided to the Eurosystem. Moreover, the Eurosystem has recently started buying ABS. The ECB ABS Purchase Programme thus further increases the total exposure of the Eurosystem to credit claims default risks.

2.2 Scope of the book

This book focuses on default models. Those can serve a variety of purposes such as assessing quantitatively the credit risk associated to the collateral pledged to the Eurosystem by its counterparties. As such, the book does not cover other models that would be necessary for the *pricing* of loans.[3]

The book targets both the broad audience, which will gain a valuable, self-contained knowledge of the models described, and the more specialist audience, which will find many relevant details about specific models including all main derivations, as well as insights into two innovative default models. The default rates models detailed in this book are not specific to credit claims, and could be applied to other asset classes such as Corporate bonds. Models for both pools of credit claims and individual credit claims – still distinguishing by sector and country – are described.

The contributions of this book are twofold. First, it reviews the standard models for estimating default rates, as well as the links between them, using homogeneous notations for their mathematical descriptions. This allows a unified presentation of most of the credit models widely used. The link between

---

[2] source: https://www.ecb.europa.eu/mopo/assets/charts/html/index.en.html#

[3] For example, it does not investigate recovery rates behaviours, or the additional subordination structures for creditor claims, or the waterfall structure for ABSs. All these layers can easily be added later, depending of the purpose of the model being built. The paper mentions some of them, when deemed relevant, but only to the extent where these concepts can be *directly* linked to the default rate modelling (for example, when time of prepayment can be made an inversely correlated quantity to the default time as in [32]).

them is often missing in the current literature, and the notations are often heterogeneous among different papers quoted in reviews. It seemed useful to have a single reference text, using the same notations across different models whenever possible, to give a good overview of the models and the links between them. Also, by emphasising each model assumptions and limitations, the book aims at providing the reader with a better understanding of each model relevance. Second, it introduces and illustrates two alternative models that could be used to advance the modelling of default. Hidden Markov chain models (HMM) allow to estimate the numerical probability of default and the credit cycle of credit claims, and is illustrated with data of some Spanish loans to Small and Medium Enterprises (SMEs). Efficient algorithms can be implemented (e.g. in Matlab) and are provided. Cox-modelling allows to extract the information content of the loan-level data stored at the European DataWarehouse and to quantify a loan's individual riskiness based on the characteristics of the obligor. It thus makes use of a massive database as well as rigorous statistical methods traditionally used in medicine, but largely unknown in Finance, to produce loan-specific relative risk assessments.

2.3 Detailed outline of the structure of the book

Section 3 describes the two families of models broadly used in Finance. It gives a precise overview of the different types of default models and highlights, whenever possible, the links between them. Each model is described such as to provide the general reader with the main intuition behind it and with the model underlying assumptions and shortcomings, while allowing the more specialist audience to understand the technical details involved. More generally, this book provides the general reader with a unified description, both in terms of terminology and in terms of mathematical notation, of the main core models of credit risk, and thoroughly explains the links between the models. To improve the clarity of the book, all mathematical derivations are placed in Annex. These derivations follow the order of the main text of the book, and should be considered as part of it. The first family consists of the so-called *structural models*, most of them, including the model used in the Capital Requirement Directive of Basel II, are derived from the Merton and Vasicek models. The second family consists of the *statistical co-dependency models*, and includes the Gaussian co-dependency model as well as its Levy process generalisation [1]. Through Monte-Carlo simulations, these approaches can be used to induce inverse correlation between default rates and prepayment rates, an interesting and realistic feature. Section 3 shows that most of the models described in this first section (the Vasicek, some specification of the

Gaussian-copula and its generalisation [1]), ultimately result in a common risk factor impacting simultaneously all the loans of the pool involved. Hence, the question of knowing what really constitutes this risk factor arises. Specifying explicitly this risk factor by using a proxy variable, or by assuming a theoretical distribution for it, or even by inferring it from asset prices, implies additional model risks. Indeed any arbitrarily chosen proxy may be inappropriate.

Section 4 explores two new and promising perspectives in default modelling, which are borrowed from other fields and adapted to the modelling of defaults. The first model is based on the theory of *hidden Markov chains*, and to the author's knowledge has only been used in the context of US corporate bonds default data [15]. Nevertheless, the model is not specific to this asset class[4]. Hidden Markov models provide a current estimate of the credit risk cycle (low or high) together with the probability of defaults in each of the period of the cycle. It does not make any assumption about the risk factor but derives it solely from the default data. Interestingly, the European Data Warehouse has been operational since January 2013, and collecting loan-level data on all ABSs pledged to the Eurosystem, as loan-level data has been made an eligibility criteria for ABSs. This data would allow in the long term, once it covers enough observations in a steady state of the economy and in a high default-risk state, to estimate directly the probability of default of a given sector/jurisdiction as well as the past and current credit cycle of a specific sector or a specific pool of credit claims, which can be different from the business cycle. Because the implementation part is far from trivial, having efficient algorithms for this purpose, properly documented, is a valuable asset. In the short-term, these algorithms are illustrated for assets for which data exists such as European corporate bonds, and some delinquency data of credit claims extracted from Bloomberg. The second model is based on the *Survival Analysis* theory, and is applied to the data of the European Data Warehouse. It uses Cox-modelling to infer the higher probability of default of a given type of loans compared to a baseline, and is applied to the loans backing ECB eligible Spanish SMEs. Because Cox-modelling allows to estimate relative risks of particular types of loans with respect to a baseline, as well as to make use of the data of delinquencies from the European Datawarehouse, it is an important model to include in any risk-modeller toolkit.

---

[4] Availability of long-enough default series data for US Corporate bonds probably explains the article main focus on this specific asset class.

2.4 Notation and preliminaries

This short section details preliminaries in terms of notations, basic probability facts, commonly used risk-measures, and discusses the concept of portfolio granularity. It is mainly needed for Section 3, which gives a broad overview of the commonly used default models. It is also useful as introductory reading for the literature of default modelling in general. The reader only interested in the alternative default models of Section 4 can skip this section and go directly to Section 4.

2.4.1 Random variables for modelling default

General preliminaries

For any random vector $X = (X_1, ..., X_k)$ we denote by F_X its (multivariate) cumulative distribution function (cdf), that is,

$$F_X(a) = P(X_1 \leq a_1, ..., X_k \leq a_k)$$

for every real vector $a = (a_1, ..., a_k)$.

If F is a multivariate cdf we often denote by F_i its ith marginal. We denote by Φ the cdf of the standard normal law, that is, the Gaussian law with mean 0 and variance 1, and by ϕ its density.

We define the inverse of a univariate cdf F by:

$$F^{-1}(a) = \inf\{t,\ F(t) \geq a\}$$

In case F is invertible then F^{-1} coincides with the usual definition of the inverse of a bijective function. For $a \in [0, 1]$, the quantity $F^{-1}(a)$ is called the a-*quantile* of the distribution. If F is the cdf of a random variable X, $F^{-1}(a)$ is also known as the a-quantile of X. If α is a expressed in percentages rather than in units (i.e. $\alpha = 100.a$), $F^{-1}(a)$ is called the α-*percentile*.

For a given asset or loan i and time t denote by $\lambda_{i,t}$ the instantaneous hazard rate of loan i at time t. It is the average probability of default of a loan which has not defaulted until time t over a very short interval of time $[t, t+dt]$, hence the name "instantaneous". The $\lambda_{i,t}$ can be a deterministic quantity, or a random variable. Let τ_i be the time of default of loan i. The τ_i are modelled as (non-deterministic) random variables. Let $PD_i(t)$ be the cumulative distribution function of τ_i, that is,

$$PD_i(t) := F_{\tau_i}(t) = P(\tau_i \leq t)$$

Intensity models

A so-called intensity model links the cumulative probability of default $PD_i(t)$ to the instantaneous hazard rate $\lambda_{i,t}$ by:

$$PD_i(t) := P(\tau_i \leq t) = 1 - \exp(-\int_0^t \lambda_{i,s}ds)$$

In case PD_i is differentiable, the above formula can be easily proved from the definition of the hazard rate (Annex 6.1).

Most of the time, the $\lambda_{i,s}$ are in fact assumed non-stochastic. They are often even assumed constant: $\lambda_{i,s} = \lambda_{i,0} =: \lambda_i$ for all borrower i. In that case the intensity model reduces to:

$$PD_i(t) = P(\tau_i \leq t) = 1 - \exp(-t\lambda_i)$$

In practice, intensity models are very useful to transform a single data point $p_{\tilde{t}}$ of the (cumulative) probability of default of debtor i over the time interval $[0, \tilde{t}]$ into a whole term-structure of the cumulative probability of default $t \to PD_i(t)$, which is a function defined on the interval $[0, T]$ and of values in $[0, 1]$, for a chosen horizon T of the model.[5] Most of the time $p_{\tilde{t}}$ is estimated from market data, using the excess spread on bonds or a Credit Default Swap (CDS) spread, or it can be taken from the rating agencies tables of probability of default, or inferred from the commercial bank borrower rating score. Deriving λ_i from $p_{\tilde{t}}$ is done by setting the empirical quantity $p_{\tilde{t}}$ equal to the theoretical quantity $1 - \exp(-\tilde{t}\lambda_i)$ where $\tilde{t}$ is the time horizon of $p_{\tilde{t}}$. For example the credit rating agencies tables indicate the cumulative probability of default for each rating class with an horizon of one year, hence $\tilde{t} = 1$. For example one can look at the most liquid CDS when such instruments are available for the borrower, and very often these are the three or five year CDS. Hence $\tilde{t} = 3$ or 5, depending of the most liquid CDS maturity. Solving for λ_i in:

$$p_{\tilde{t}} = 1 - \exp(-\tilde{t}\lambda_i)$$

yields

$$\lambda_i = -\frac{\ln(1 - p_{\tilde{t}})}{\tilde{t}}$$

Admittedly, other methods exist to derive the curve $t \to PD_i(t)$, for example using bonds of different maturities. In the context of credit claims from small

---

[5]This is simply the restriction to the interval $[0, T]$ of the cumulative distribution function of τ_i, the time of default of loan i.

2.4. NOTATION AND PRELIMINARIES

borrowers, this is often not possible, hence a one point estimate $p_{\tilde{i}}$ is first used to infer λ_i, and then the whole curve $t \to PD_i(t)$ is derived through the intensity model using the inferred λ_i.

Two simple mathematical facts are constantly used in the context of default modeling and simulations:

Lemme 1 *Let U be a uniformly distributed variable on $[0, 1]$. Let F_X be the cumulative distribution function of some random variable X. Then $F_X^{-1}(U)$ follows the same law than X, that is, $F_{F_X^{-1}(U)} = F_X$.*

Proof. $P(F_X^{-1}(U) \leq a) = P(U \leq F_X(a)) = F_X(a)$ for any real a since $F_X(a) \in [0, 1]$. ∎

Lemme 2 *Let X be a random variable and F_X its cumulative distribution function. Then $F_X(X)$ is uniformly distributed on $[0, 1]$.*

Proof. $P(F_X(X) \leq a) = P(X \leq F_X^{-1}(a)) = F_X(F_X^{-1}(a)) = a$ for any real a, by definition of F_X. ∎

Commonly used risk-measures

The Value at Risk (VaR) at the α confidence level of a given risky asset (which can be an individual asset or a portfolio), denoted by VaR(α), is the αth percentile[6] of the risky asset loss distribution L:

$$\text{VaR}(\alpha) = \inf\{l,\, P(L \leq l) \geq \alpha\} = F_L^{-1}(\alpha)$$

Intuitively, one could expect that the losses on the asset value would not exceed the VaR(α) of the asset more than $1 - \alpha$ percent of the time[7], since VaR(α) is the smallest l such that $P(L > l) = 1 - P(L \leq l) \leq 1 - \alpha$. The VaR has remained a widely used measure of risks among portfolio managers; Bassel II also uses the VaR(0.999) for defining its capital requirements. Nevertheless, it has two main drawbacks: it says nothing about the size or average size of the extreme losses of the αth percentile, and it is in general not subadditive,

---

[6] When the loss distribution is not continuous, its upper α quantile $\inf\{l \,|\, P(L \leq l) \geq \alpha\}$ could be higher than its lower α quantile $\inf\{l \,|\, P(L \leq l) > \alpha\}$. We will (arbitrarily) always opt for the upper quantile, which is more conservative as losses are counted positively ($L \geq 0$).

[7] Note that such frequency interpretation, to be valid, implicitly needs the rather unrealistic assumption that no auto-correlation exists in the sequence of losses. The correct mathematical interpretation is the probabilistic one.

meaning the Value at Risk of a portfolio can be more than the sum of the values at risk of its individual components.

The Expected Shortfall (ES) at the α confidence level is simply the average loss conditional on the losses being in the worse α quantile[8]:

$$ES(\alpha) = E(L \,|\, L \geq \text{VaR}(\alpha))$$

Alternatively, it can be proved[9] that:

$$ES(\alpha) = \frac{1}{1-\alpha} \int_\alpha^1 \text{VaR}(u) du$$

As an example of its use, the Expected Shortfall at the 99% confidence level is the chosen Eurosystem tail risk measure. In particular, this is the measure used to calibrate the haircuts on the collateral the Eurosystem receives from the counterparties participating in refinancing operations. Setting the haircut equal to the Expected Shortfall at the 99% confidence level insures that, in expectation, the Eurosystem will make a zero loss even if all the losses realisations are drawn from the worse percentile of the tail distribution of losses. Contrary to the VaR, it can be proved that the Expected Shortfall is subadditive [23]. By definition, it also gives a good indication of the size of the average loss in the worse αth percentile.

Notice that the VaR and the ES only depend on the loss distribution L of the considered asset, hence they are sometimes defined in relation to the loss distribution L only, with no mention of the underlying portfolio.

2.4.2 Granularity of a portfolio and Herfindahl index

Intuitively, the concept of granularity refers to the extent to which a system can be broken into smaller parts, or that a larger entity can be subdivided. Granularity is certainly relevant in a risk management context. If the system is "granular", the aggregate risk of the portfolio depends less on individual, idiosyncratic shocks, as no single loan is given an extreme weight in the overall

---

[8] This is in fact the definition of the Tail Conditional Expectation, to which the Expected Shortfall is equal in case of a continuous distribution. The interested reader can refer to [23] for the general (and cumbersome) definition of Expected Shortfall and its comparison to Tail Conditional Expectation. When no distinction needs to be made for the purpose of the present paper we always present the simplest definition.

[9] This general fact is admitted here. For a proof the reader can refer to Acerbi and Tasche (2002), "On the cooherence of expected shortfall" J Bank Fin 26 (7), page 1492.

2.4. NOTATION AND PRELIMINARIES

portfolio risk. Hence, a granular portfolio risk would be mainly driven by the common factors which affect all the loans simultaneously than by individual loan characteristics. The Herfindahl index, which we define below, is a measure of granularity commonly used by market participants.

Let consider a portfolio of n loans and let $w_{i,t}$ be the share of the ith loan in the total loan amount at time t. The Herfindahl index at time t is, by definition:

$$H\,\mathrm{erf}_t = \sum_{i=1}^{n} w_{i,t}^2$$

Notice low values of the index indicate higher granularity.

2.4.3 Definitions of defaults

The notion of default is given very different definitions depending on the overall context, type of asset and jurisdiction. For example, in the Basel II framework defaults are usually defined as the event of the borrower being more than 90 days late in a payment to the creditor, or being unlikely to pay. But in the case of retail (including credit card) and public sector entities exposures, the 90 days figure can be replaced by figures up to 180 days. National discretion lists provided by national supervisors indicate the cases where a bank should apply a longer than 90 days definition for the event of default on certain products[10]. Rating agencies have a different approach. Both Standard and Poor's and Moody's characterise default as encompassing any missed or delayed disbursement of interest and/or principal, bankruptcy, and distressed exchange[11]. Hence rating agencies do not allow for a potential grace period after a missed or delayed payment, contrary to Basel II and most bank internal default accounting.

Overall, for Corporates the definitions in use are usually inspired by the rating agencies and thus more or less consistent, whereas for retail there is a variety

---

[10] See the Basel Committee on Banking Supervision FAQ, http://www.bis.org/bcbs/qis/qis3qa_f.htm.

[11] As an example, Moody's definition of default for Corporate includes three types of credit events:

1. A missed or delayed disbursement of interest and/or principal;
2. Bankruptcy, administration, legal receivership, or other legal blocks (possibly by regulators) to the timely payment of interest and/or principal; or
3. A distressed exchange occurs where: (i) the issuer offers debt holders a new security or package of securities that amount to a diminished financial obligation (such as preferred or common stock, or debt with a lower coupon or par amount, lower seniority, or longer maturity); and (ii) the exchange has the effect of allowing the issuer to avoid a bankruptcy or payment default. See for example "Corporate Default and Recovery Rates", 1920-2008, page 51.

of different definitions. A practical consequence is that it can be more reliable to use data concerning delinquencies than data concerning events classified as defaults for quantitative studies. For example, the three month delinquency rate is the percentage of loans of a pool which are more than three months late in repayment of principal or interest, and provides a much more homogeneous statistic across jurisdictions than defaults[12].

---

[12] Homogeneity across jurisdictions is one of the two reasons some modellers actually use delinquency data, and not default data, to project defaults. The other reason is often simply the data quality of the time series themselves. A model for translating delinquencies into defaults is then required.

Chapter 3

Description of main default models

3.1 Structural models

3.1.1 The Merton model

Model description [28]

Simply put, Merton model (1974) assumes that a firm will default if, at the time of servicing its debt, the value of its assets stands below the value of its debt. The Merton model of default is considered to be the first modern model of default. It originally applies to a *single* borrower i. Still, for consistency of notations with the next sections, as well as for the extension to multi-borrowers in this section, we will indicate the index i on each variable involved. Merton model is called a *structural* model, or *asset value* model, because the probability of default PD_i of the borrower i is directly linked to the evolution of the value of its assets $A_{i,t}$ and of its debt $B_{i,t}$. The model was originally formulated for corporate debt. The intuition underpinning Merton's reasonning is the following: at maturity T of the debt, which is modelled for simplicity as a zero-coupon bond of value $B_{i,t}$, the shareholders of the company can decide whether or not to honour their obligations by paying back their debt. If the value of the firm is below the value of the debt $B_{i,T}$ of the company at time T, the shareholders will not repay and let the company default. Bondholders will be entitled to liquidate the company assets and will share the profits from the sale, whereas shareholders will make a zero profit. If the value of the firm is above the debt level $B_{i,T}$ of the company at time T, then the firm will repay. Hence, Merton simple model sees the shareholders as having a European call option on the firm's assets with maturity T (the maturity of the debt) and strike price $B_{i,T}$ (the value of the debt at time T). The shareholder's payoff at time T is thus:

$$\max(0, A_{i,T} - B_{i,T})$$

where $A_{i,t}$ is the value of the firm at time t and $B_{i,t}$ the debt level of the firm at time t. This allows Merton to use the framework developped by Black and Scholes for option pricing [5].

It is important to understand Merton's original idea since it leads to the broader concept of a threshold $B_{i,T}$ under which default occurs. In the more advanced models which are detailed below, this threshold will be time varying, the quantity $A_{i,T}$ which is compared to it will not necessarily be a function of the value of the debtor assets, and defaults will be allowed to occur at any time t instead of just at maturity of the debt T. Nevertheless, the idea of a threshold to which some creditworthiness index of the firm compares still forms the basis of most default models.

The value $A_{i,t}$ of the borrower's assets being not observable[1], a model for its evolution has to be assumed. Merton assumes that $A_{i,t}$ follows a Ito stochastic process of the form:

$$dA_{i,t} = r_i A_{i,t} dt + \sigma_i A_{i,t} dW_{i,t}$$

This allows Merton to directly use Black and Scholes framework for option pricing, in which the probability of default is:

$$PD_i = P(A_{i,T} < B_{i,T}) = P(Y_i < c_i) = \Phi(c_i)$$

where

$$c_i = \frac{\ln(B_{i,T}) - \ln(A_{i,0}) - r_i T + \frac{\sigma_i^2}{2} T}{\sigma_i \sqrt{T}}$$

and Y_i is a standard normal random variable. The derivation is presented in Annex 6.2. Because default is triggered in scenarios where the realisation of the variable Y_i is below the value c_i, the variable Y_i can be seen as indicating the borrower credit-worthiness: the higher it is, the more credit-worthy the borrower. For this reason we will from now on call Y_i the *credit-worthiness index* of loan i. Notice Merton model implies a standard normal distribution for Y_i, as indicated above.

---

[1] Even for listed companies, all that can be observed are the stock exchange values. Those are often taken as a proxy for the value of the firms itself, but this is an approximation.

3.1. STRUCTURAL MODELS

Limitations, extensions and current use

In this section we explain the limitations of the Merton model [28], and how they were dealt with by the financial industry. The proposed extensions to the Merton model pave the way for the joint simulation of default covered in the next section, such as the Vasicek one-factor model [35].
The main limitations of the simple Merton model are the following:
1) it is a *one-period default model*, or a *static* model: although the dynamics of Y_i follows a continuous time-process on $[0, T]$, default can only occur at time T in the model;
2) the process driving the value $A_{i,t}$ of the firm i is not observable;
3) it is a *single-borrower* default model;
4) the debt structure assumed for the firm is very simple (a zero coupon bond), and refinancing conditions are not taken into account in the model;
5) it does not take into account liquidity effects on the default of firms.

Despite these limitations, two widely used model of credit risk, CreditMetrics^{TM} and KMV^{TM}, both rely on the Merton model.
CreditMetrics^{TM} was developed in 1997 by the risk management research division of JP Morgan, which eventually became the RiskMetrics^{TM} group. The quality of its publicly available methodology description [12], stemming from the philosophy of its authors[2] to make the product transparent, contributed to its success and influence in many bank-internal developments of credit risk models. The CreditMetrics^{TM} approach is used by many central banks [4], either directly using the CreditManager software, or through in-house systems developed in Matlab or Excel using a similar methodology.
KMV was a small company who specialised in credit and portfolio tools which was acquired by Moody's. Most of large banks and insurance companies use at least one of the major KMV products.

The first limitation was addressed as early as 1976 by Black and Cox [6] extension of the model. It simply consists in assuming that default occurs as soon as the value of the assets falls below the debt threshold. Hence the time of default τ_i of the ith borrower is just $\tau_i := \inf\{t, A_{i,t} < B_{i,t}\}$. For that reason, it is called a *first-passage* model. Defaults can take place at any time, and using properties of the brownian motion such as the reflection principle allows to derive a closed analytical formula for the default probability during any time interval. Nevertheless, this is at the cost of a higher mathematical

---

[2] The authors were Gupton, Finger and Bhatia, although the technical note has been improved, as well as the underlying methodology, many times since its first issue in 1997.

complexity. Moreover, it introduces the problem of the predictability of default: because the underlying asset value process is a continuous process (with no jumps), and that default occurs only when this process hits the level of the default threshold, default does not come as a surprise, in contrast to what usually happens in real situations. Attempts in the financial literature to tackle the predictability of default in first-passage models have consisted either of incorporating jumps in the value process $A_{i,t}$, which can thus unexpectedly fall below the default threshold [19], [37], or by allowing only for imperfect information from the lender side, who will not know the exact position of the process $A_{i,t}$ anymore, and thus can be surprised by the borrower default [10], [17], [25].

Concerning the second limitation[3], notice that what is really required in the model is an estimation of the credit-worthiness process Y_i. Although this estimation stems from the value of the firm in Merton's original model, with underlying dynamics given by the stochastic process $dA_{i,t} = r_i A_{i,t} dt + \sigma_i A_{i,t} dW_{i,t}$, other specifications for Y_i can be used. For example, CreditMetrics^{TM} make the variable Y_i linearly dependent on a vector of factors X, as decribed in Annex 6.3. The parameter c_i can then be calibrated based on the empirical probability of default PD_i by noticing that $PD_i = \Phi(c_i)$ implies $c_i = \Phi^{-1}(PD_i)$. Notice that estimating the c_i in that way also allows to address the fourth limitation, as the debt level B_t completely disappears from the model[4]. Nevertheless, this is at the cost of the loss of the dependence of default on the current debt level that was in the original Merton model. Hence, the influence of the borrower debt level on its probability to default will only be taken into account insofar his debt level is already captured through the empirical PD_i (or by the borrower rating used to derive the PD_i). Similarly, the refinancing conditions are only taken into account in this model insofar they are captured by PD_i[5].

---

[3] Admittedly, when the borrower is a company publicly traded, the Merton model can be calibrated using stock prices by solving a system of two equations. One is the price of the equity as implied by this model, which considers equity as a call option, and results from the Black and Scholes formula, and the other stems from an application of Ito's lemma. In the context of credit claims such information is not available, and hence not developed further in the present paper. The interested reader can refer to Hull [24], page 490.

[4] Admittedly, there had been other attempts to introduce more complex debt structures than a simple zero-coupon bond, such as Geske multi-coupon debt [14] where the decision to default or not is taken at each coupon payment date. The main common problem of these models is the calibration. Even if calibration were correct they would be very firm-specific and unusable in practice from a comprehensive, global risk-management perspective.

[5] Because most of the time these probability of default estimates are backward-looking (eg realised default frequencies from rating agencies tables), a change in the access to liquidity of the borrower is thus *completely neglected* by all the default models based on Merton's

3.1. STRUCTURAL MODELS

Similarly, the third limitation can be addressed within the framework of Merton model by specifying *dependent, inter-related* processes Y_i for each borrower i. Different default thresholds c_i can still be set for each borrower, depending on their credit quality rating, but the dependence introduced between the dynamics of the credit-worthiness indexes Y_i will induce correlation in the joint modelling of the borrowers defaults. Hence, the Merton model already yields a pool default model when the driving processes of the borrowers' asset values are made co-dependent. It is precisely the specification of different, yet inter-related processes Y_i for each borrower i which opens the door to the Vasicek default models for *pools* of loans explained in the next section (Section 3.1.2).

An illustration of the use of the Merton model by CreditMetrics^{TM} is provided in Annex 6.3. The KMV^{TM} methodology is roughly similar and hence omitted in the present book. Asset correlations between the different counterparties are solely captured by the stock price correlations of the respective composite indices the borrowers are mapped to. Indeed, each borrower, be it listed on a stock exchange or not, is mapped, depending on both its industry and country, to a different index[6]. Notice also correlation is not estimated directly in the model, but will result from the correlations between the synthetic stock market indices created for each borrower.

3.1.2 The Vasicek one-factor model for pools

Model description

The Vasicek one-factor model was one of the first models proposed for modelling defaults in *pools* of loans. It was presented by Vasicek in its seminal paper [35] as linked to the Merton [28] structural model. Nevertheless, as we will see, the asset dynamics can be taken out of the model easily, and realised default taken as an input. The only assumptions still shared with the Merton model will be the concept of thresholds under which the loans default, on the one hand, and the probability distribution of the credit-worthiness variables involved, on the other hand. We choose to present here this shorter version

---

approach. This model drawback has thus potentially contributed to the mis-pricing of risk preceding the financial crisis.

[6] The index can be a synthetic one made of different existing broad market indexes, depending on the borrower industry participation and the jurisdiction of the market it operates in. For example, a borrower might be mapped as 80% French and 20% Germany, and as 70% chemicals and 30% finance, resulting in its reference index being 56% French chemicals, 24% French finance, 14% German chemicals and 6% German finance. See Table 8.8 and 8.9 of [12], p 94-95.

of the Vasicek model, but the interested reader can refer to Annex 6.4 for the link between the Vasicek and the Merton's structural model.

The Vasicek model consists in assuming that each firm i is associated to a variable Y_i indicating its credit-worthiness and that this variable Y_i can be written as:

$$Y_i = \sqrt{\rho}Z + (\sqrt{1-\rho})\epsilon_i$$

where Z and the ϵ_i are mutually independent, identically distributed random variables following a standard normal law. Note that, by independence, the Y_i are themselves Gaussian, of variance 1 and expected value 0.

Default of firm i occurs in the time period $[0,T]$ if the realisation of the variable Y_i is below the Merton's threshold c_i. The formula giving c_i in terms of the parameters of the Merton model is given in Section 3.1.1 and is proved in Annex 6.2. But most of the applications of the Vasicek model do not model explicitly c_i. Instead, they use the following shortcut: Merton's relation states that $\Phi(c_i) = PD_i$. Hence, if PD_i is an (unconditional) probability of default of loan i, then c_i can be recovered by: $c_i = \Phi^{-1}(PD_i)$. This way of only *partially* using some underlying structural model results is typical of the field of default modelling. We will find similar transformations using the inverse quantile function in, for example, the copula approach (Section 3.2).

Hence, the unconditional probability of default of loan i becomes:

$$PD_i = P(Y_i < c_i) = P(Y_i < \Phi^{-1}(PD_i))$$

Borrowers do not default independently from one another, as all the Y_i are impacted by the same common risk factor Z. From independence of the Z and the ϵ_i, it is trivial to see that $Cor(Y_i, Y_j) = \rho$ for all $i \neq j$.

Assuming a portfolio from which all loans are of equal size and whose number of loans tends to infinity, and that all loans have the same probability of default $PD_i = PD$, Vasicek proves that the distribution of the pool default ratio is:

$$P(L \leq x) = \Phi(\frac{\sqrt{1-\rho}\Phi^{-1}(x) - \Phi^{-1}(PD)}{\sqrt{\rho}})$$

The proof is given in Annex 6.5. It relies on the fact that conditional to the realisation of the common factor, the variables Y_i are independent, and thus the Law of Large Numbers can be applied to find the limiting distribution.

Vasicek model belongs to the class of so-called *one-factor conditionally independent default models*, since, conditional to the realisation of the single common systematic risk factor Z, all the Y_i, and hence all the defaults, are

3.1. STRUCTURAL MODELS

independent. Not only this is a crucial fact used for the derivation of the above formula giving the distribution of losses of the portfolio, but it allows to easily compute the Value at Risk and the Expected Shortfall of the portfolio, through a similar limit argument, as the idiosyncratic components factor out in the limit.

Calibration and current use

The Vasicek one-factor model is often used in conjunction with Gordy's framework [18]. This is because under a certain set of technical conditions, but with very broad assumptions in terms of individual probability of default, of loss given default and of loan size distribution, Gordy provides a formula for the portfolio loss distribution, its Value at Risk as well as its Expected Shortfall (Annex 6.6). Notice Gordy's framework still requires that the Herfindahl index[7] of the porfolio tend to 0 when the number of loans tends to infinity, a condition already mentioned in Vasicek original work [35]. Hence, Gordy's framework is very similar to Vasicek's framework in the sense that the loss distribution is derived asymptotically, meaning that in practice it only holds for a "very large" number of loans.

The Vasicek model is used to derive the conditional probability of default which is then plugged into Gordy's formula. The derivation[8] is detailed in Annex 6.6. We describe below one of the most important application of this composite approach.

3.1.3 The Gordy/Vasicek model and Basel II capital requirements

The very core of the Internal Rating Based (IRB) approach of Bassel II to obtain the levels of regulatory capital relies on the mixed Vasicek/Gordy framework described above. Basel II requires banks to hold a minimum level of capital, also referred to as regulatory capital. The more risky a bank's assets, the higher the value of the regulatory capital it should hold. Basel II allows banks, subject to a certain number of conditions, to use the IRB approach

---

[7] As explained in Section 2.4.2, the Herfindahl index is a measure of the granularity of a portfolio.

[8] Contrary to the other derivations found in Annex, this proof is not self-contained as it starts from one of the main result from Gordy [18] and proceeds to describe what we believe are *the most meaningful steps* of the mixed Gordy/Vasicek approach. The reader interested in the proof of the (here admitted) technical preliminary result can refer to [18] or [23].

to derive their level of capital requirements[9]. Basel II[10] divides a bank's assets into five asset classes: corporate, sovereign, bank, retail and equity[11]. It considers each of this asset class as forming a separate portfolio, and uses the Vasicek/Gordy model to derive the amount of regulatory capital to be held to cover for the risk of each of these portfolios. Hence, the total amount of regulatory capital is simply the sum of the amounts to cover each asset class portfolio. The capital required by each of these five asset classes is the VaR at the 99.9% confidence level as expressed in Annex 6.6 and indicated below; LGD_i is the random variable representing the loss given default of loan i, and w_i the assumed fixed portion of loan i as a percentage of the total nominal amount of the portfolio:

$$VaR(\alpha) = \sum_i w_i E(LGD_i \,|\, Z = F_Z^{-1}(1-\alpha))\Phi(\frac{\Phi^{-1}(PD_i) + \sqrt{\rho_i}\Phi^{-1}(\alpha)}{\sqrt{1-\rho_i}})$$

The final capital requirement slightly differs from this exact formula as:
- the unexpected loss, defined as the difference between the VaR and the expected loss, is considered in place of the single VaR, so as to account for the provisioning of the non-performing loans expected to default;
- the expected loss given default factor $E(LGD_i \,|\, Z = F_Z^{-1}(1-\alpha))$ is approximated by an expected loss given default in "severe economic downturn";
- the one-year probability of default PD_i is scaled for loans of longer maturity, a process called *maturity adjustment*;
- the result from the formula is multiplied by a *scaling factor* equal to 1.06 based on a quantitative impact study[12].
These adjustments are described in more detail in [23].

The individual probability of default PD_i, the expected loss given default as well as the exposure at default are all inputs provided by the bank itself or

---

[9] An incentive for banks to implement this approach as opposed to the standard Basel approach is that the resulting regulatory capital is generally lower.

[10] See the Basel Committee on Banking Supervision document: "International convergence of capital measurement and capital standards: a revised framework" [3], paragraph 215 to 243.

[11] Within the corporate asset class, five sub-classes of specialised lending are separately identified. Within the retail asset class, three sub-classes are separately identified. Within the corporate and retail asset classes, a distinct treatment for purchased receivables may also apply provided certain conditions are met. For the purpose of ease of explanation, only five classes with no subclasses and no exceptions are mentionned here.

[12] 365 banks participated in the study, which focuses on the impact of Bassel II in terms of capital requirement as compared to Bassel I.

given by the regulatory rules[13]. The internal model is assessed by national regulators. Another important parameter input of the Vasicek model are the correlations ρ_i. The Basel II framework assumes the following, empirically-based estimation of the correlation coefficient:

$$\rho_i = 0.24 - 0.12 \frac{1 - \exp(-50 PD_i)}{1 - \exp(-50)}$$

Limitations of the Gordy/Vasicek model

In both applications, asset correlations are introduced to obtain stressed values of the probability of default through the use of a Vasicek model applied to the pool of all assets from the same sector. Hence the correlations ρ_i which appear in the formulas of the model are not correlations between the different assets of the pool considered (the pool of all the bank lendings in the case of Basel II), but correlations on all existing similar assets. They are used to obtain stressed probability of defaults, probably to capture the impact of (unknown) common factors on the default probabilities of similar loans.

Moreover, both approaches assume an infinitely granular portfolio, and hence can only in practice be applied to very granular portfolio.

3.2 Statistical models

All the previous models are labelled as *structural*, as they are assuming some type of underlying process related to the borrower's fundamentals which explains (triggers) the borrower's default. Another approach avoids modelling the reasons of the defaults, but instead focuses solely in reproducing a given default pattern. The models resulting from this approach are often called *statistical* default models.

3.2.1 The copula approach

The most commonly used statistical default model for pools of loans are *copula-based models*. Copulas are useful as they are mathematical tools which allow to capture virtually any type of dependence between the loans' defaults. That being said, in most applications a specific type of dependence is assumed through the *Gaussian copula*. Another advantage of copula models is that they are *dynamic* models of default in the sense that default can occur at any

---

[13] More precisely, in the *advanced IRB approach*, all those paramteters have to be estimated by the bank, whereas in the *foundation IRB approach*, the loss given default is given by the regulatory rules.

time. This is particularly relevant for pricing instruments whose values are dependent on a pool of loans such as ABSs, as the timing of defaults becomes very important in that context.

General model description

A copula can be simply defined as the joint distribution function of random variables uniformly distributed on the interval $[0, 1]$:

Définition 1 *A function $C : [0,1]^k \to [0,1]$ is a (k-dimensional) copula if there exist k random variables $U_1,...,U_k$ uniformely distributed on $[0,1]$ such that C is their joint distribution function, idem est such that:*

$$C(u_1, ..., u_k) = P(U_1 \leq u_1, ..., U_k \leq u_k) \quad \text{for all } (u_1, ..., u_k) \in [0,1]^k$$

The use of copula functions to model joint probability distributions is theoretically justified by Sklar's theorem:

Théorème 1 *Let $F = F_{(Y_1,...,Y_k)}$ be a k-dimensional cdf, and F_i its marginals. Then there exists a k-dimensional copula C such that:*

$$F(y_1, ..., y_k) = C(F_1(y_1), ..., F_k(y_k))$$

Moreover, there is unicity of the copula on the cartesian product of the ranges of the F_i.

In particular, Theorem 1 implies the unicity of the copula associated with F when each of the marginals F_i are continuous. Note the *existence* part of the theorem is easy to prove as setting $u_i := F_i(y_i)$ allows to write:

$$\begin{aligned} F(y_1, ..., y_k) &= P(Y_1 \leq y_1, ..., Y_k \leq y_k) \\ &= P(Y_1 \leq F_1^{-1}(u_1), ..., Y_k \leq F_k^{-1}(u_k)) \\ &= P(F_1(Y_1) \leq u_1, ..., F_k(Y_k) \leq u_k) \end{aligned}$$

Because each $F_i(Y_i)$ is uniformly distributed by Lemma 2, let $U_i := F_1(Y_1)$, and let

$$C(u_1, ..., u_k) := P(U_1 \leq u_1, ..., U_k \leq u_k)$$

This gives the relevant copula.

Hence a copula can model virtually any kind of dependence between random variables.

3.2. STATISTICAL MODELS

Strictly speaking, a k-dimensional cdf F is entirely defined by its copula C and its marginal densities F_i. This is because, as seen in the proof above:

$$F(y_1, ..., y_k) = C(F_1(y_1), ..., F_k(y_k)) \quad (1)$$

And by Sklar theorem, the converse is true on the cartesian product of the ranges of the marginals: the cdf F entirely defines the copula as

$$C(u_1, ..., u_k) := P(F_1(Y_1) \leq u_1, ..., F_k(Y_k) \leq u_k) \quad (2)$$

Relations (1) and (2) are very important for understanding the use and simulations of random variables through the copula approach.

Quantile-to-quantile correspondence

A copula allows to model the joint probability of uniform random variables U_i. Hence it is natural to look for a model of joint default where the U_i would *somehow* represent the time of default τ_i. Because the U_i are all related to each other through the copula which generates them, this would allow to obtain correlated variables for the time of default of the diverse loans of the pool. Nevertheless the times of default variables τ_i probably do not follow a uniform distribution. Moreover, the cumulative distribution functions of time of default $PD_i(t)$ are inferred from borrower credit score or market data as explained earlier, and a good modelling requires using those curves $PD_i(t)$ – possibly different for each borrower – as an input to the copula model. Ideally, a joint modelling of the probabilities of default of the pool loans should be consistent with the empirically determined marginal distribution functions $PD_i(t)$. That is, the model should not impose additional structure on the marginal times of default than the $PD_i(t)$ curves previously determined through the intensity model, and should yield precisely those marginal probabilities of default. **The main interest of the (general) copula approach is precisely that it allows to specify *any* dependence structure between the time to default while being compatible with *any* given unconditional (i.e. marginal) individual loan distribution of default.**

Recall that PD_i is the cumulative distribution function of the time of default τ_i of loan i and define $U_i := PD_i(\tau_i)$. By Lemma 2, U_i is uniformly distributed. Hence, the copula approach can be followed, but with $U_i = PD_i(\tau_i) = F_i(Y_i)$ (see proof of Theorem 1). This correspondence is called quantile-to-quantile correspondence, as $y_i = F_i^{-1}(PD_i(e_i))$ is a correspondence which allows to go from a realisation of the empirical distribution e_i to a realisation of the theoretical one (given by the copula) y_i. Notice this correspondence can be set between virtually *any* empirical or inferred distribution PD_i to any distribution F_i. Hence the choice of the copula is absolutely unconstrained by the PD_i.

The Gaussian copula, and other types of families

From relation (2) define a *Gaussian* copula as a copula satisfying:

$$C(u_1, ..., u_k) := P(F_1(Y_1) \leq u_1, ..., F_k(Y_k) \leq u_k)$$

where the F_i are the marginals associated to a k-variate Gaussian cumulative distribution F. Without loss of generality[14], we can assume the F_i to be all standard normal Gaussian variables: $F_i = \Phi$ for all i. Similarly, one can define other types of copulas, depending on the family of the multidimensional probability distribution functions being considered, such as Student's t-copula and Archimedean copulas, which include the Gumbel copula. The interested reader can refer to [16], chapter 17, page 333, for a precise description of those families.

The Gaussian one-correlation parameter copula model

Li's [27] proposes Gaussian copulas as a mean to systematically model credit risk. The Gaussian one-correlation parameter copula model is a particular case of Gaussian copula still widely used by the financial industry. It is defined as a Gaussian copula $C(u_1, ..., u_k) := P(F_1(Y_1) \leq u_1, ..., F_k(Y_k) \leq u_k)$ with the additional property that

$$Corr(Y_i, Y_j) =: \rho, \text{ for all } i \neq j$$

It can easily be shown that it can be simulated from the following model:

$$Y_i = \sqrt{\rho}Z + (\sqrt{1-\rho})\epsilon_i$$

where Z and ϵ_i are mutually independent, identically distributed standard normal Gaussian variables, and default has occurred at time t for borrower i whenever t satisfies:

$$Y_i < F_i^{-1}(PD_i(t))$$

The variable Y_i can be interpreted as the credit-quality of loan i, which is influenced both by an idiosyncratic factor ϵ_i, and by a systematic factor Z

---

[14]This is the consequence of the fact that copulas are invariant by transformation of the marginals by increasing functions. Because the functions $y \to \frac{y-\mu}{\sigma}$ are increasing and transform a normal law of mean μ and variance σ^2 to a standard normal Gaussian law, the result follows.

3.2. STATISTICAL MODELS

which affects all the loans of the portfolio. Notice that by independence of Z and ϵ_i, the two-dimensional random vectors (Z, ϵ_i) are Gaussian, and hence the variable Y_i is also Gaussian. Also, the variable Y_i is compared to the *default threshold* $a_i(t) := F_i^{-1}(PD_i(t))$, in a way similar to the Vasicek one-factor model. This is the reason why the variable Y_i is sometimes called a *credit-worthiness indicator*, as in [32]: when it falls below the threshold, the associated loan defaults.

Since by Lemma 2 the variable $F_i(Y_i)$ is uniformly distributed, it follows that

$$P(Y_i \leq F_i^{-1}(PD_i(t))) = P(F_i(Y_i) \leq PD_i(t)) = PD_i(t)$$

as wanted. Hence only the *joint* probability of default depends on the copula, and the unconditional probability of default matches exactly the empirical input $PD_i(t)$.

The time of default random variable τ_i is thus simply the function which solves:

$$Y_i = F_i^{-1}(PD_i(\tau_i))$$

That is,

$$\tau_i = PD_i^{-1}(F_i(Y_i))$$

Notice τ_i is both a function of the empirical curve $t \to PD_i(t)$ and of the copula since $U_i := F_i(Y_i)$ is the uniform random variable which is the ith marginal of the copula[15].

3.2.2 Lévy process approach

As a generalisation of the Gaussian one-correlation parameter model

Before introducing the Lévy process approach proposed in 2008 by Dobransky and Schoutens [1], notice that the previous Gaussian one-factor framework consists in assuming the following model for the credit-worthiness of the loan i:

$$Y_i = X_\rho + X_{i,1-\rho}$$

where X_ρ and $X_{i,1-\rho}$ are independent random variables, X_ρ follows a Gaussian distribution of mean 0 and variance ρ and the $X_{i,1-\rho}$ are identically distributed

---

[15]Hence, to obtain a realisation t_i of the time of default of the ith borrower, that is, a realisation of the random variable τ_i, all that is needed is to obtain a realisation u_i from the copula marginal distribution U_i. Then the time of default is derived as $t_i = PD_i^{-1}(u_i)$. The way copulas are simulated depends on their nature. The Gaussian copula is particularly easy to simulate: just simulate Z and ϵ_i as defined above, and get $U_i := F_i(\sqrt{\rho}Z + (\sqrt{1-\rho})\epsilon_i)$.

and follow a Gaussian distribution of mean 0 and variance $1 - \rho$. It follows that
$$Corr(Y_i, Y_j) =: \rho, \text{ for all } i \neq j$$

The model

The one-factor Lévy process framework from Dobransky and Schoutens [1] is simply a generalisation of the above Gaussian framework: instead of using a Gaussian distribution for the processes X_ρ and $X_{i,1-\rho}$, another Lévy process is chosen. Construction and description of Lévy processes is outside the scope of the present book; the interested reader could refer to [11] for a comprehensive description of these interesting processes which allows for "jumps", a very interesting feature.

Example of a drifted Gamma process

As an illustration of a particular type of Lévy process different from a Gaussian one, we consider here a drifted Gamma process as in [1], which finds Gamma processes are more appropriate process than Gaussian processes for modelling defaults in Collateralised Debt Obligations (CDO). The model can be written as:
$$Y_i = X_\rho + X_{i,1-\rho}$$
with X_ρ and $X_{i,1-\rho}$ are defined by
$$\begin{aligned} X_\rho &= \sqrt{a\rho} - G_\rho \\ X_{i,1-\rho} &= \sqrt{a(1-\rho)} - G_{i,1-\rho} \end{aligned}$$
where G_ρ and $G_{i,1-\rho}$ are independent random variables following different Gamma distributions: the variable G_ρ follows a Gamma distribution of parameter $\rho a > 0$ and $b = \frac{1}{\sqrt{a}}$, while the variables $G_{i,1-\rho}$ follow a Gamma distribution of parameter $(1-\rho)a > 0$ and $b = \frac{1}{\sqrt{a}}$. Other processes, in particular Poisson processes with unexpected jumps, could be used.

Recall that the density function of a Gamma distribution $\mathcal{G}(a,b)$ of parameter $a > 0$ and $b > 0$ is defined by:
$$f(x;a,b) = \frac{b^a}{\Gamma(a)} x^{a-1} \exp(-xb)$$
with $\Gamma(a)$ such that
$$\int_{-\infty}^{+\infty} f(x;a,b)dx = 1$$

3.2. STATISTICAL MODELS

As in the Gaussian case, the model assumes default at time t if, and only if, the credit-worthiness index falls below some *default threshold* $a_i(t)$. To calibrate this default threshold, the default probabilities under this model are matched against those empirically obtained, that is, the theoretical probability of default $P(Y_i \leq a_i(t))$ of the model is set equal to $PD_i(t)$[16], in the same way that would be done for a Gaussian copula.

$$P(Y_i \leq a_i(t)) = PD_i(t)$$

is successively equivalent to:

$$F_{Y_i}(a_i(t)) = PD_i(t)$$
$$a_i(t) = F_{Y_i}^{-1}(PD_i(t))$$

The time of default for loan i is thus obtained, as in the Gaussian approach, by solving

$$Y_i = F_{Y_i}^{-1}(PD_i(t_i))$$

That is,

$$t_i = PD_i^{-1}(F_{Y_i}(Y_i))$$

---

[16] As explained in section 2.4.1, $PD_i(t)$ was obtained from the intensity model calibrated with the empirical, point in time data p_T.

Chapter 4

Alternative default models

4.1 Hidden markov chain models

4.1.1 Motivation

In all the models described in the previous section, correlation between defaults is introduced, explicitly or implicitly, by the mean of a "common risk factor", which is assumed to weigh on the creditworthiness of all the borrowers in the pool at the same time. This common factor can be estimated directly from the macroeconomic variables deemed relevant, as in a one-factor model CreditMetrics framework, or be assumed to follow a given theoretical probability distribution, as in the Vasicek one-factor model. The correlation parameter, in any case, is simply the dependence of the creditworthiness of the borrower, and hence of his probability of default, to the common factor[1]. When an attempt is made to specify the common factor, an issue arises. If the common factor is assumed to follow a (theoretical) probability distribution, which probability distribution should be chosen? The Vasicek one-factor model and the Gaussian copula model choose a normal distribution. If on the contrary the common factor is assumed to depend on observable macroeconomic data, the issue of correctly selecting the relevant explanatory variables arises. When the focus is shifted away from the identification of the common factor to the correlation factor, the problem simply translates into the issue of estimating this correlation factor.

A Hidden Markov chain Model (HMM) consists of an unobservable Markov

---

[1] Admittedly, using industry and country specific factor loadings, CreditMetrics allows to go farther than the framework of a single *one*-factor model. Nevertheless, even then, it does not calibrate the model on actual defaults, but on stock market indices which are assumed to represent the (hidden) firm value process as in a Merton's model.

chain which determines the risk-state of the economy. The risk-state influences the individual and/or collective loan probability of default. Hence, in a HMM, correlation between the loans' defaults is induced only by the common factor, which is the hidden risk state. In this sense, HMM models are similar to many of the models detailed in the first section, be it the Vasicek model (Section 3.1.2), the Gaussian copula model (Section 3.2), or the generalisation of the copula approach with Lévy processes (Section 3.2.2). As explained earlier, all these models indeed introduced correlation in the default events through a single unobserved common factor. The rationale for using HMM models in estimating default rates is that it does not need to make any assumptions on the possible set of variables driving the common factor, nor on the common factor distribution. The common factor is determined *endogenously from the default data* by maximum likelihood techniques. In particular, it could be that the credit cycle follows different dynamics than the usual macroeconomic variables that we associate with expansions and recessions like GDP growth[2]. In that case, HMM will allow to get to very different results in terms of probability of default estimations compared to any other model based directly on macroeconomic variables, as it will allow a default-cycle to be fit to the data, which can then be used for predictions. Admittedly, a k-state HMM only allows the common factor to take k distinct values. But these values do not appear as numerical values in a default triggering inequality as in the case of the previous models reviewed. Instead, each value for a "HMM common factor" determines another "state" of the economy, in which *any* probability distribution of default can be assumed.

In this section we provide an illustration of the use of the HMM approach in a way similar to [15], but on European default data.

4.1.2 Description of the two-states binomial HMM and implementation

In a two-state HMM, the risk-state of the economy is modelled via two different (unobserved) states: a *low risk state*, labelled 1, and an *high risk state*, labelled 2. The risk state determines the probability distribution of defaults. Loans are assumed to default independently conditional to the risk state. They are also assumed to be so similar than they have the same probability of default.

---

[2]For an example of how the credit cycle of a specific industry can differ substantially from the overall economy business cycle (as defined by the IMF), the reader can refer to the US Energy sector study performed in [15]. Assuming a higher probability of default for the energy companies in the index during recessions would lead to results opposed to reality, as the two cycles are almost completely disjoint.

4.1. HIDDEN MARKOV CHAIN MODELS

Hence if p_i is the individual loan probability of default in a given state i in $\{1,2\}$, the law governing the number of defaults $\tilde{O}_t$ at time t is simply the binomial distribution:

$$P(\tilde{O}_t = k) = \binom{n_t}{k} p_i^k (1-p_i)^{n_t-k}$$

where n_t is the number of bonds in the sample at time t, and k any integer in $\{1, ..., n_t\}$. We will call this model a *binomial two-state HMM*. In the high risk state the individual probability of default p_2 is expected to be higher than in the low risk state.

Very often time series of defaults are only available through the time series of the corresponding default *rates*. A way to use the two-states binomial HMM described above in the case of default *rate* series is to assume that the default rate multiplied by some (high enough) constant n and rounded to the closest integer corresponds to the number of actual individual defaults of some (proxy) portfolio of constant size $n_t = n$. Hence it is assumed that there exists some portfolio for which if k loans default on a given period, k new loans of similar risk-profile are introduced before the start of the next period. Admittedly, this approach may fail to provide some useful information about the loans' default behaviour compared to a "real default data series" approach. Nevertheless, empirically we did not find any significant difference between the two models. The reason might be that the number of defaults being usually low compared to the overall size of the sample, working with a decreasing sample size or on the default rate series is roughly equivalent.

The transition from state i to state j is governed by the *state transition matrix* $A = (a_{ij})$, where a_{ij} is the probability of moving to state j, conditional to being in state i. Given an observation sequence $O_1...O_T$, where for each t in $\{1, ..., T\}$ the number O_t is the realisation of the random variable $\tilde{O}_t$ defined as the number of defaults at time t, the model is re-estimated repeatedly until the log-likelihood of observing $O_1...O_T$ is maximised.

After estimation, retrieving the implied "most-likely" state sequence can be done using the Viterbi algorithm which finds, through dynamic programming, the single state sequence with the highest probability of occurring among all state-sequences of length T. Alternatively, it can be done by maximising the expected number of correct states, an algorithm which makes use of some previously computed quantities of the estimation, and that we choose to call the *HMM algorithm* for state-retrieval[3]. Both state-retrieval algorithms outputs depend not only of the observation sequence but also on the estimated

---

[3] The two approaches do not theoretically necessarily yield the same result. In practice we noticed the state sequences retrieved closely resemble each other.

parameters of the model. The converse does not hold: retrieving the state sequence is only an additional analysis which does not affect in any way the fitted parameters of the model.

There are three main issues in the practical implementation of HMMs: the efficiency of the algorithms used, underflow[4], and the non-global character of the maximum likelihood estimates found which makes them depend on the assumed initial conditions.

Efficient algorithms we borrow from the Speech Recognition literature [33] and we implement in Matlab. These algorithms involve computing the log-likelihood, given the model, using the so-called *forward* and *backward* paths, which contrary to direct computation results in an efficient (i.e. polynomial time in input size) algorithm. The methodology used in the illustration contained in this book is explained in detail in Annex 7.1.1.

For the computation of forward and backward paths underflow is dealt with by rescaling the corresponding quantities by an appropriate factor, at each step, after verifying that the re-scaled parameters satisfy the recursive relation of the efficient algorithm. For the Viterbi algorithm, underflow is simply dealt with by taking the logarithms.

The possible existence of different (local) maxima is dealt with by perturbing the initial conditions in an *ad-hoc* manner. This is by no mean a complete answer to the problem, but can certainly allow detecting instable solutions, that is, local maxima which depend very much on the starting point used for the parameter estimations.

To provide an illustration and a better understanding of the methodology as well as a performance check of the (non-trivial) algorithms involved, we apply it to data simulated by a binomial two-state HMM. This simulated example is detailed in Annex 7.1.7.

4.1.3 European speculative grade corporate defaults

The data sample consists of 12 month trailing default rates, at a monthly frequency, of European speculative grade corporates bonds, as provided by Moody's on its website[5]. The default rate series was converted into a synthetic bond sample as explained in Section 4.1.2, using a factor $n = 1000$, meaning there are at each time period 1000 bonds in the sample and that the first period number of defaults is 48 (corresponding to the rate of default of 4.8%).

---

[4]Underflow occurs when the quantities computed become so small that they are (wrongly) assimilated with 0 in the machine memory.

[5]www.moodys.com

4.1. HIDDEN MARKOV CHAIN MODELS

The sample starts on January 1999 and ends on January 2013. The speculative grade corporate bonds follow a credit cycle more closely related to individual corporate loans than investment grade corporate bonds. Hence, they are taken here as a proxy for corporate loans. Nevertheless, drawback of this time series with respect to HMM are twofold.

First, it is a trailing rate, meaning the series is bound to exhibit persistence, and the fitted HMM will reflect this persistence. Hence, if the goal is to predict future defaults, using point in time (in this case, monthly) default rate would have been more appropriate.

Second, it does not distinguish between the different sectors (consumer, etc.) and thus is not granular enough to be useful for estimating precisely credit claims probability of defaults, for example. The aggregation potentially explains that the high risk states seem distinguishable by simple graphical inspection of the data time series, without requiring the more sophisticated use of HMM to uncover them.

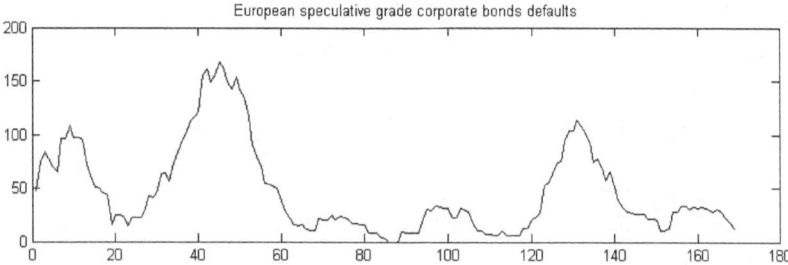

Figure 4.1: 12 month trailing default series on all European speculative grade bonds rated by Moody's

Initial values for the estimation are fixed in the most objective way as possible as follows: the initial probability distribution is $\pi = (0.5, 0.5)$. This means, we assume there is no more chance to be in state 1 than in state 2. Also, we assume that in each state there is an equal chance to move to the other state, that is, the initial state transition matrix is:

$$A = \begin{bmatrix} 0.5 & 0.5 \\ 0.5 & 0.5 \end{bmatrix}$$

Concerning the individual loan probability of default in the low risk state and the high risk state, they are fixed the following way: according to the initial distribution and transition probability indicated above, there is a 50% chance of being in state 1 and a 50% chance of being in state 2. More precisely by the property of Markov chain such an initial chain would be 50% of the time in state 1 and 50% of the time in state 2. The average probability of default is thus $\frac{1}{2}p_1 + \frac{1}{2}p_2$, which we make equal to the realised frequency of default of the sample. We then just need to specify the ratio $\frac{p_2}{p_1}$ and the values of both p_1 and p_2 will be determined. We decide to choose $\frac{p_2}{p_1} = 2$, which is the single arbitrary choice in our initial guess. The table below indicates the initial guess, and the parameter estimates obtained after 100 iterations to maximise the log-likelihood.

	initial guess	parameter estimates
π_1	0.5	1
π_2	0.5	0
p_1	0.0315	0.0206
p_2	0.0629	0.0922
a_{11}	0.5	0.9810
a_{22}	0.5	0.9523

The results are interesting. The maximum likelihood estimation has separated further two risk-state and has fully characterised them. The initial ratio of 2 between the low and high risk state was not a local maxima and has been increased as high as $\frac{0.0922}{0.0206} = 4.4757$. Hence probability of default appears in this sample very much dependent on the state, which gives credit to muti-state models for defaults. Similarly, the permanence of being in a given risk-state and hence the "inertia" of the model has been increased, from the null inertia we started with (as in any given state we assumed a 50% chance to go to the other state) to as high as 98%, for the low risk state, to 95% for the high risk state. Hence in a low risk state there is only a 2% chance to go to a high risk state, and from a high-risk state there is a 5% chance to go to a low risk state.

Figure 4.2 below indicates the default series and the underlying retrieved state sequence. The Viterbi algorithm and the HMM algorithm happen to retrieve the same state sequence of low and high default states.

The goodness of fit of the model can be assessed through the computation of the so-called mid-pseudo residuals (see Annex 7.1.5). If the fitted model is correct, these residuals should be standard normal. Figure 4.3 below indicates, from top to bottom and left to right: the data series of the residuals of our simulation, their fit vis-a-vis of the standard Gaussian law via a histogram and a quantile-to-quantile plot, as well as their partial autocorrelation function (PACF). As indicated earlier in HMM models it is perfectly normal for residuals to be correlated: this does not have negative implications for the adequacy of the model.

4.1. HIDDEN MARKOV CHAIN MODELS

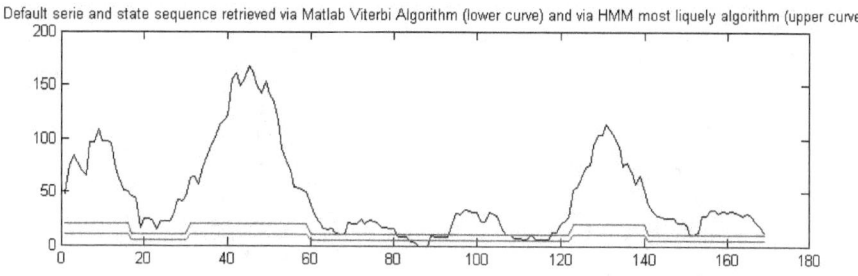

Figure 4.2: Default series and retrieved state sequence

Furthermore, normality tests can be carried out on these pseudo-residuals. For example, Jarque-Bera normality tests reject the null of a standard Gaussian for the mid-pseudo residuals at the 10% confidence level, but not at the 5% level.

One can also use parametric bootstrap to obtain the standard deviation as well as the variance-covariance matrix of the estimated parameters. Parametric bootstrap is described in Annex 7.1.3. The set up is the same as explained in Section 7.1.7, and we obtain the following correlation matrix:

	p_1	p_2	a_{11}	a_{22}
p_1	1	0.0091	0.1181	−0.1253
p_2		1	−0.0564	0.1351
a_{11}			1	−0.1531
a_{22}				1

as well as the mean and standard deviation of each parameter. The table below reports the previously indicated fitted model (which generates the scenario for our bootstrap), the means of the different parameters of the fitted models and their standard deviation.

	parameter estimates	mean parameter estimate	standard deviation
p_1	0.0206	0.0206	0.0005
p_2	0.0922	0.0920	0.0015
a_{11}	0.9810	0.9788	0.0147
a_{22}	0.9523	0.9340	0.0445

Figure 4.4 below indicates the empirical parameter distribution obtained for each of the fitted parameter p_1, p_2, a_{11} and a_{22}. As can be seen from the top

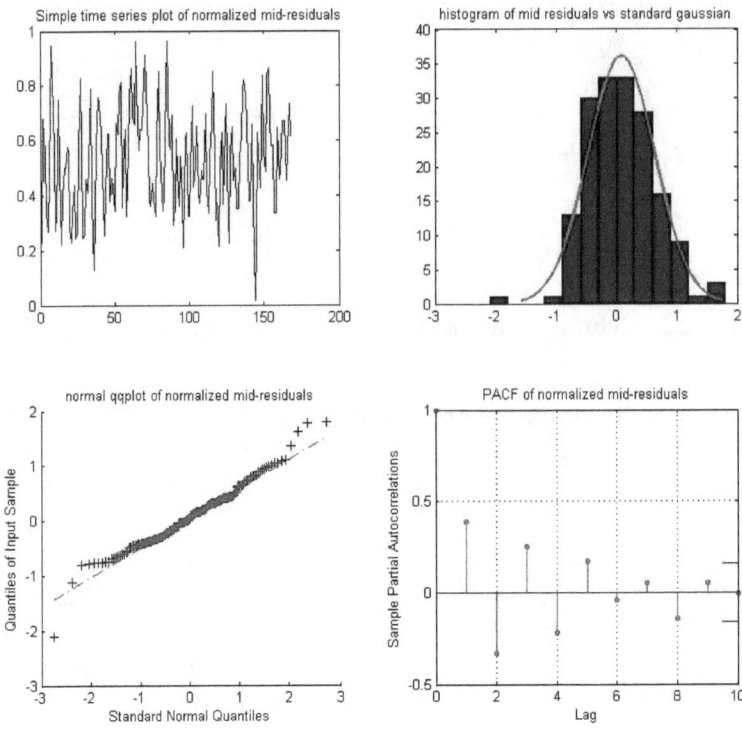

Figure 4.3: Analysis of the goodness-of-fit of the model for corporates using mid-pseudo-residuals

two histograms, p_1 and p_2 cannot reasonably be assumed normally distributed. Nevertheless they seem more concentrated around the mean than a normal law. Hence we can deduce a 95% confidence interval as (less than) 1.96 times the standard deviation: $p_1 = 0.0206 \pm 0.0005$ and $p_2 = 0.0922 \pm 0.0015$. As the upper bound for p_1 (0.0211) is lower than the lower bound for p_2 (0.0907), we would say that the two distinct states are well identified (at a 95% confidence level).

4.1.4 European pool data from Bloomberg

To be useful for the practical purpose of assessing the probability of defaults of credit claims, there is the need for credit claims default series data. A minimum requirement on the data is that it should be split by type of loans, as

4.1. HIDDEN MARKOV CHAIN MODELS

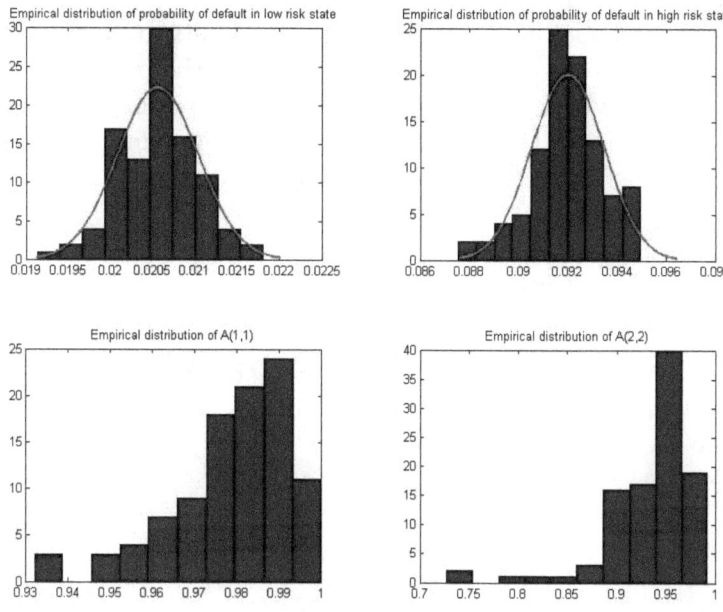

Figure 4.4: Empirical estimates dispersions

for example mortgage loans have a very different risk profile than, say, loans to Small and Medium Enterprises (SMEs). Also, divergence in overall European country risk profiles as well as difference in national legislation concerning loans indicate that country-specific indexes are needed, at least for a risk analysis purpose.

Default data is in general very difficult to obtain. Rating agencies do possess such series but regard them as highly propietary. Defaults are rare events, hence a long enough serie, or a large enough sample, is required to perform precise HMM analyses and uncover risk states and conditional default probabilities. The new European DataWarehouse recently started providing loan-by-loan data, including default, for all Eurosystem eligible ABSs. As pools of credit claims constitute the underlying backing ABSs, this data will provide a valuable source of defaults for the assessment of the risk of credit claims in general.

Currently, this data is not available with a sufficiently long history. We obtained instead the one month delinquency rate for pools of credit claims backing eligible ABSs from Bloomberg. Observations can date back as far as to

2006. This is unfortunately no loan-by-loan-level data, but it provides the percentage of default of the pool in percent of the nominal outstanding the pool, at each point in time[6]. We aggregated this data over all the pools of a given country and asset class at each point in time, weighted by the proportion of the pool outstanding amount to the overall outstanding amount of all ABSs, to obtain our generic default rate indexes (using delinquencies as a proxy for defaults).

We chose here to illustrate the HMM methodology on Spanish SMEs. The data is presented in Figure 4.5 below.

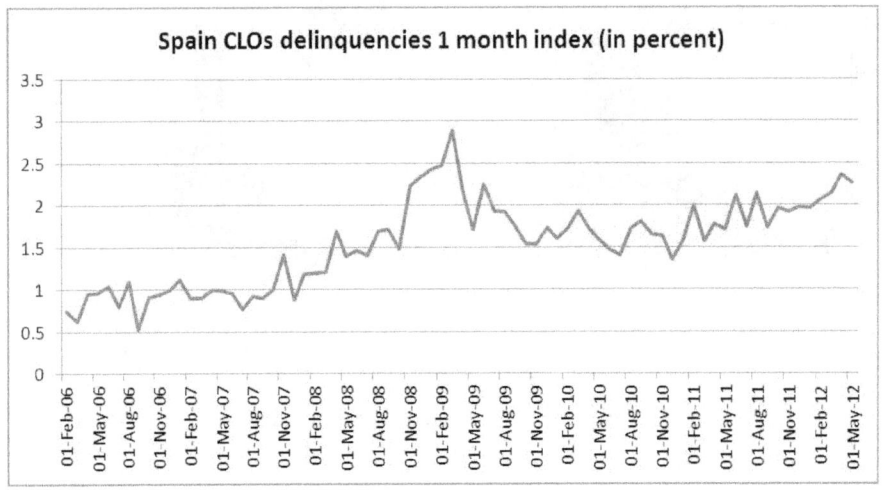

Figure 4.5: Spain CLOs one month delinquencies

Initial values for the estimation are fixed in the same way as in the previous section (Section 4.1.3). The parameter estimates are reported in the table below, together with the initial values assumed:

	initial guess	parameter estimates
π_1	0.5	1
π_2	0.5	0
p_1	0.0100	0.0091
p_2	0.0200	0.0179
a_{11}	0.5	0.9613
a_{22}	0.5	1.0000

---

[6] Admittedly, this is not quite the same as the percentage of defaults in terms of number of loans, with the exception of the particular case where all loans would be of the same size.

4.1. HIDDEN MARKOV CHAIN MODELS

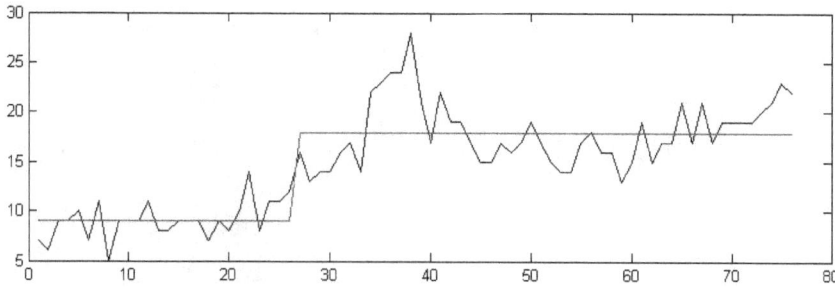

Figure 4.6: Default series with retrieved state sequence.

The results are interesting. The maximum likelihood estimation has separated further two risk-state and fully characterised them. The initial ratio of 2 between the low and high risk state was almost a local maxima and has only been decreased to $\frac{0.0179}{0.0091} = 1.967033$. Probabilities of default are, for this sample, very much dependent on the state. Similarly, the permanence of being in a given risk-state and hence the "inertia" of the model has been increased, from the null inertia we started with (as in any given state we assumed a 50% chance to go to the other state) to as high as 96%, for the low risk state, to 100% for the high risk state. This 100% probability was estimated because the sample only exhibits a single change from state 1 to state 2. Hence it does not provide the HMM with any information about the possibility of leaving the high risk state, and in consequence the HMM indicates a structural change, as it predicts the new high probability of default will persist indefinitely.

Figure 4.6 below indicates the default series and the underlying retrieved state sequence. Notice the Viterbi algorithm and the HMM algorithm retrieve the same state sequence of low and high default states.

The goodness of fit of the model can be assessed through the computation of the so-called mid-pseudo residuals (see Annex 7.1.5). If the fitted model is correct, these residuals should be standard normal. Figure 4.7 below indicates, from top to bottom and left to right: the data series of the residuals of our simulation, their fit vis-a-vis of the standard Gaussian law via a histogram and a quantile-to-quantile plot, as well as their partial autocorrelation function (PACF). Notice in HMM models it is perfectly normal that residuals be correlated: this does not have negative implications for the model.

Furthermore, normality tests can be carried out on these pseudo-residuals. For example, Jarque-Bera normality tests reject the null of a standard Gaussian

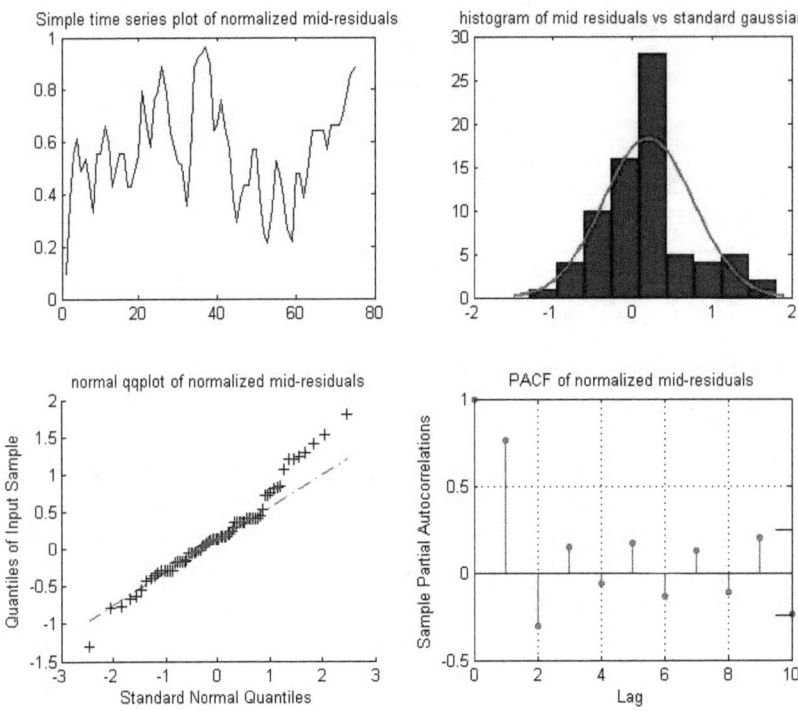

Figure 4.7: Analysis of the goodness-of-fit of the model for Spanish CLOs using mid-pseudo-residuals

for the mid-pseudo residuals at the 10% confidence level, but not at the 5% level.

One can also use parametric bootstrap to obtain the standard deviation as well as the variance-covariance matrix of the estimated parameters. Parametric bootstrap is described in Annex 7.1.3. The set up is the same as explaned in Section 7.1.7, and we obtain the following correlation matrix:

	p_1	p_2	a_{11}	a_{22}
p_1	1	0.1073	−0.3755	−0.0587
p_2		1	−0.0915	0.7561
a_{11}			1	−0.0149
a_{22}				1

A very strong positive coefficient (75%) is found between p_2 and a_{22}. This indicates that the results at this level should be taken with caution: the parameters do not seem uniquely determined.

We also obtain the mean and standard deviation of each parameter. The table below reports the previously indicated fitted model (which generates scenario for our bootstrap), the means of the different parameters of the fitted models and their standard deviation.

	parameter estimates	mean parameter estimate	standard deviation
p_1	0.0091	0.0094	0.0017
p_2	0.0179	0.0176	0.0015
a_{11}	0.9613	0.8770	0.1831
a_{22}	1.0000	0.9523	0.0148

Figure 4.8 below indicates the empirical parameter distribution obtained for each of the fitted parameter p_1, p_2, a_{11} and a_{22}. As can be seen from the top two histograms, p_1 and p_2 cannot reasonably be assumed normally distributed. They seem much more concentrated around the mean than a normal law. Hence we can deduce a (conservative) 95% confidence interval as (less than) 1.96 times the standard deviation: $p_1 = 0.0091 \pm 0.0017$ and $p_2 = 0.0179 \pm 0.0015$. As the upper bound for p_1 (0.0108) is lower than the lower bound for p_2 (0.0164), we conclude that two risk states are indeed disentangled.

4.2 Cox-modelling of default rates

4.2.1 Motivation

Extracting default data from loan-level data of ABS

Loan-level data of pools backing eligible ABS has recently become available to the Eurosystem and private investors alike through the European DataWarehouse. Because eligibility criteria of ABS as collateral for the Eurosystem monetary operations now include loan-level data reporting, many deals have been reported to the European DataWarehouse by Eurosystem counterparties. Currently the loan-level data quality is not high enough to allow any kind of estimation. For example, estimating realised loss-given-default for mortgage loans does not yield convincing results at the current juncture. Defaulted loans are flagged in the data which would suggest that Probability of Defaults (PDs) could be estimated based on realised defaults. Nevertheless, estimations of those PDs in terms of levels are low compared to both banks internal rating (IRB) systems for the same types of loans and to rating agencies estimates by

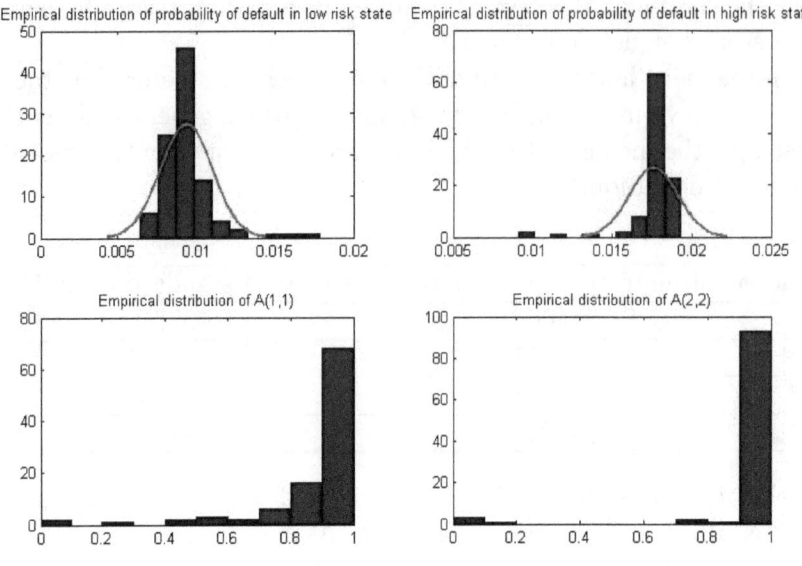

Figure 4.8: Empirical estimates dispersions

sector. This is probably mostly due to a significant reporting bias: older loans having defaulted before the start of the reporting period were not required to be reported, for operational and practical reasons. Only those loans who defaulted after the start of the mandatory reporting period *had to* be reported as such in the template. Although counterparties were encouraged to also report previous defaults, it is clear that any estimation of PDs based solely on loan-level data runs the risk of being significantly biased downwards.

In this section we apply Survival Analysis, a well-established branch of Statistics used in the pharmaceutical and in the medical industry, to extract as much default information from the loan-level data as possible. More precisely, the methods borrowed from Survival analysisallow us to quantify the increase in risk due to certain loan individual characteristics as reported in the loan-level data fields compared to some *baseline loan characteristics*, whose probability of default is left un-estimated. For example, we find that a Spanish SME loan whose purpose is reported as "Debt-consolidation" has twice a higher default rate than when it is reported as "Purchase" in the loan-level data, controlling for all other relevant loan-level data fields as well as for a selected set of macroeconomic variables.

4.2. COX-MODELLING OF DEFAULT RATES

Survival analysis as a tool for modelling relative default risks

Survival Analysis is a branch of statistics developed specially to estimate time to some well-defined events, called *failures*. As an established statistical theory it contains a wide battery of tests and diagnosis checks. It is applied all around the globe in order to test statistically the effects of drugs, medical processes, surgeries, etc. while controlling for other relevant variables. Understanding the default event of a loan as a failure, that is, as the event of interest, allows us to use this theory for default probabilities estimations. To our knowledge, Cox-models have never been applied to loan-level data to this date.

There are numerous advantages of using Cox regressions instead of the more classical models such as least squares regressions and logistic regressions:

- **Cox regressions make a better use of all information available at any point concerning the loan defaults**. Indeed, simple ordinary least square or logistic regressions need the explained variable - here the survival time - to be fully observed, that is, that the precise outcome (the loan did not default or the loan did default) be stated correctly for each subject in the sample[7]. But the outcome cannot be observed for loans (i) still current, or (ii) having matured during the study period. This is the reason why some restricted, shorter time-frame (e.g. one year) is usually chosen and the probability of default estimated on this restricted period (e.g. the one-year probability of default): it allows to discard less information than estimating longer periods PDs. Nevertheless much information is still discarded. In the commonly used one-year PD estimation, a lot of information is lost by scaling down the multi-year PD of cohorts defaulting after the first year in order to get a one-year estimate. In a Kaplan-Meier estimate, on the contrary, the whole information concerning the timing of failure enters the likelihood function which ends up being maximised. Hence, no information is thrown away.

- A statistical assumption needed for ordinary linear regressions is the normality of errors. In many settings linear regressions happen to be, in practice, relatively robust to deviations from normality. Nevertheless distribution of time to a given event of interest, like default, is certainly not symmetric, may be bimodal, etc., and linear regressions are definitely not robust to these deviations. On the contrary, **assumptions needed for Cox-regression are minimal**. In particular, there is no normality assumption for the distribution of errors[8], and independence of default for the derivation of the maximum

---

[7]That is, it does not allow for right-censoring. Admittedly, there exist ways to deal with right-censoring (e.g. censored-normal regressions).

[8]In a fully-parameterised model the assumption on errors is that they follow a Gumbel distribution – skewed to the right and more adequate for modelling defaults; in a semi-parametric model there is simply no assumption needed on errors.

likelihood estimator is only needed conditionally to fixing the covariates.
- **The theory allows for adjustment** for a given covariate, the use of stratification, etc. thus making different categories along a given risk factor comparable even if the values of other risk factors differ.
- **Bias in the level of the defaults** is a current issue with loan-level data. Many defaulted loans are simply not reported in the loan-level data. Nevertheless, by using Cox semi-parametric approach, we only assess risks of a given cohort *relatively to others*, and not the default level itself. Hence, we can obtain interesting insights concerning the main risk factors of defaults even if the level of default is biased downward.

4.2.2 Survival analysis modelling of the hazard rate

Survival analysis attempts to model directly the *instantaneous hazard rate* $\lambda_{i,t}$ introduced in Section 2.4.1 and elaborated upon in Annex 6.1 by assuming it can be written in a split form as the product of: (i) a function of study time, that is, the age of the loan, t; and (ii) a function of the N covariates $x = (x_k)_{k=1..N}$ of the model and their corresponding parameters to be estimated $\beta = (\beta_k)_{k=1..N}$. Hence if $x^i = (x_k^i)_{k=1..N}$ are the covariate vectors corresponding to loan i characteristics, the instantaneous hazard rate $\lambda_{i,t}$ of loan i can be written:

$$\lambda_{i,t} = \lambda_{i,t}(x^i, \beta) = \lambda_0(t) r(x^i, \beta)$$

Without loss of generality we can assume $r(\mathbf{0}, \beta) = 1$, where $\mathbf{0}$ denotes the zero vector. The function $\lambda_0(t)$ is then uniquely defined and is called the *baseline hazard function*. We make no attempt to estimate the baseline function, hence following a *semi*-parametric approach. All hazard functions relate to the baseline function multiplicatively, and hence all hazard functions also relate to each other multiplicatively, and independently of time: the ratio of two hazard functions

$$\frac{\lambda_{i,t}(x^i, \beta)}{\lambda_{j,t}(x^j, \beta)} = \frac{\lambda_0(t) r(x^i, \beta)}{\lambda_0(t) r(x^j, \beta)} = \frac{r(x^i, \beta)}{r(x^j, \beta)}$$

is independent from time. This explains the term of *proportional hazards* coined for this broad class of models.

Cox [8] was the first to propose such a model in 1972. More precisely, as a hazard rate must always be positive, Cox proposes to model linearly the logartithm of $r(x^i, \beta)$ as:

$$\ln(r(x^i, \beta)) = \langle x^i, \beta \rangle = x_1^i \beta_1 + x_2^i \beta_2 + ... + x_N^i \beta_N$$

4.2. COX-MODELLING OF DEFAULT RATES

Parameters $\beta = (\beta_k)_{k=1..N}$ are determined using maximum likelihood techniques. The derivation of a form of a "partial likelihood" [8] which allows estimation of the parameters $\beta = (\beta_k)_{k=1..N}$ without having to estimate the baseline hazard function is out of the scope of the present book. The interested reader can refer to [21] for more details. What is crucial is to know that both uncensored observations, that is, observations that defaulted during the study period, and uncensored ones, contribute to the likelihood.

The focus of Survival Anlaysis is often the so-called survival function, defined as

$$S_i(t) = P(\tau_i > t) = 1 - P(\tau_i \leq t) = 1 - PD_i(t)$$

As shown in Annex 6.1, $PD_i(t) = 1 - \exp(-\int_0^t \lambda_{i,s} ds)$, which provides a direct link between survival functions and hazard rates:

$$S_i(t) = \exp(-\int_0^t \lambda_{i,s} ds)$$

Censored observations contribute to the likelihood as $S_i(t)$, hence all information contained in the fact that they did not default during the study period is taken into account (contrary to loggit regressions for estimating one-year probability of default for example). Uncensored observations contribute by their density $PD'_i(t)$.

4.2.3 Modelling choices

Jurisdiction-specific models

Preliminary analyses of the impact of various loan-level variables on realised default rates indicate that these impacts vary significantly depending on the jurisdiction. This is most probably because bank practices for granting loans to SMEs differ across jurisdictions. Hence, it is more prudent to try to isolate jurisdiction-specific explanatory variables of default, or *risk-factors*[9]. Moreover, not only does the jurisdiction affect the explanatory power of the variables, but it also impacts the explained variable itself. This is due to two main reasons: first, what constitutes a default is jurisdiction specific: there is not a uniform definition of default across all jurisdictions. Second, the way defaults are recorded in the loan-level data probably also depends on the jurisdiction. Building a single model for all countries would introduce a heterogeneous bias in the recording of realised defaults.

---

[9] Because including country dummies and all the interaction terms between the country dummies and the other risk factors would result in a very large number of predictors, it is preferable to build country-specific models for default rates.

Definitions used for the modelling

We define defaults at the loan-level from loan-level data exclusively. A loan is said to be in default if it is in default according to the "transaction default definition" of the loan-level template (about 31509 defaults for the whole SME sample as of July 2014) or if it is more than 90 days in arrears, in principal or repayment (an additional 17908 loans for the whole SME sample). In that second case we deduce the date of default by subtracting from the current snapshot date the number of days in arrears and adding 90 days. This stricter definition of defaults allows being more forward-looking by including in the analysis the loans which may not yet legally be considered as defaulted. It also mechanically provides more defaults for our estimations.

We define *analysis time* as calendar time minus the origination date of the loan. Analysis time is a very important concept for Survival Analysis as it differs from calendar time, that is, the real date of the records found in the loan-level data. Analysis time thus simply corresponds to the *age of the loan* if the loan is still outstanding and observed. Age is a crucial explanatory variable for default, since empirically the hazard rate of loans is not constant over time. It is thus interesting to make age a main dimension of our analyses in predicting defaults by our very definition of analysis time.

To apply Survival Analysis to the modelling of default, we have to define a link between the event of "success" or "failure", as well as to define what are the censored observations. We use the following "paradigm": *"All loans default eventually. The loans whose defaults are not observed in the sample are right-censored observations. Censoring occurs either because a loan is still outstanding and non-defaulted or because it has matured before defaulting."*

Pre-selection of loan-level data explanatory variables

For each of the potential candidates as explanatory variables for the default rate among the 138 fields of the SME loan-level template, we apply univariate analysis to pre-select a subset of explanatory variables. More precisely, we consider in turn:

(i) simple histograms of the number of realised defaults;
(ii) similar histograms of the average PD given by the counterparty IRB system, as reported in the SME loan-level template;
(iii) more advanced Kaplan-Meier estimates of curves of realised defaults as a function of loan age;
(iv) log-rank or Cox-Wilson univariate tests of equality of survivorship functions.

4.2. COX-MODELLING OF DEFAULT RATES

Because this analysis remains exclusively univariate, it is akin to try to find risk factors by dividing the sample population across different "strata" and comparing the number of defaults in each "strata". Because a given risk factor may be made redundant once another more relevant risk factor, or combination of risk-factors, is included, all the risk factors deemed relevant by the results from our univariate analysis do not necessarily qualify for being included as explanatory variables in the final, multivariate model.

Various reasons can lead to discard otherwise promising explanatory variables: too many missing values (NAs), too different group sizes, non-statistical significance, and, one one occasion (Originator name), crossing survival curves that are not compatible with the proportional hazard rate assumption made in Cox-modelling. Different values of a loan-level data field are regrouped when there is no sensible univariate difference between the two groups in terms of defaults, in view of the analyses above (i) to (iv). Results are reported in the table below:

Loan-level data variables	result of univatiate analysis
Obligor legal form or business type	regrouped and retained[10]
Customer segment	*discarded*
Borrower Basel III segment	kept as such[11]
Origination year	*discarded*
Final maturity date	*discarded*
Seniority of the loan	*discarded*
Interest payment frequency	*discarded*
Amortiation type	*discarded*
Payment type	*discarded*
Weighted Average Life of the loan	*discarded*
Collateral type	regrouped and retained[12]
Originator name	not used[13]
Purpose	regrouped and retained[14]
Type of loan	*discarded*
Is it a floatting rate?	regrouped and retained[15]
Current rate margin	retained

---

[10] We formed the following groups: (A) base case: Public Company (1), Limited Company (2) and Partnership (3); (B) Individual (4) and Other (5). We deleted the NAs.

[11] Each of the borrower basel III segment on the loan-level data template was kept as a separate group: Corporate (1) as the base case, SME treated as Corporate (2), Retail (3), and Other (4); NAs were deleted.

[12] We defined Residential properties (14) as the base case; all other 22 collateral types were regrouped together, including the NAs.

[13] All 8 main SME ABS originators in Spain are present in the "Originator Name" loan-level data field. Corresponding sub-branches are in "Originator" field. Because the univariate survival curves for different originators cross each other, it is not advisable to include the field as an explanatory variable. Models with frailty will compensate for the lack of this otherwise important explanatory variable.

[14] We defined the following groups: (A) Purchase (1) as the base case; (B) Investment Mortgage (11), Re-mortgage (2), Re-mortgage with Equity Release (8), Re-mortgage on different terms (9); (C) Debt consolidation (7); (D) (12) Working Capital, ND No data; (E) Other (13), Construction Real Estate (5), Construction Other (6), Renovation (3).

[15] We derived the following groups: (A) Floating rate loan (for life) (1), Floating rate loan linked to Libor, Euribor, BoE reverting to the Bank's SVR, ECB reverting to Bank's SVR (2), Fixed rate loan with compulsory future switch to floating (5), Capped (6), Discount (7), Switch Optionality (8), Borrower Swapped (9), Other (10); (B) Fixed rate loan (for life) (3), Fixed with future periodic resets (4).

4.2. COX-MODELLING OF DEFAULT RATES

Bloomberg indices considered
Gross Domestic Product[16]
Unemployment[17]
Unemployment rate change[18]
Consumer confidence[19]
Business confidence[20]

Time-varying covariates

Although it is possible to build a model for the hazard rate of Spanish SME loans backing SME ABS using exclusively loan-level data, such a model would have only a very limited predictive ability, as some variables recognised as significant explanatory variables for the modelling of defaults such as GDP, unemployment, etc., are not available from the loan-level data alone. Nevertheless, the model built on loan-level data alone could be a "through-the-cycle" model for the baseline default distribution. Indeed, if explanatory loan-level data variables (such as interest rate type, etc.) are more or less independent from non-loan-level explanatory variables (such as GDP, unemployment, etc.), then the estimation results will reveal the relative risks of a given type of loan compared to other types of loan over the whole credit-cycle.

We present here the results where we also include other broad macroeconomic variables, which are not from the loan-level data, such as: GDP growth, the unemployment rate change, consumer confidence, and business confidence.

Frailty model

The basic idea underlying frailty models is to incorporate an unmeasured "random" effect in the hazard function to account for subject heterogeneity. Shared frailty models using the ISIN name to regroup loans of the same pool are thus similar to Fixed Effect panel regressions on the pools and can be thought of as having a shared hazard ratio for each loan belonging to the same pool. We chose to employ shared frailty models because the originator name and the origination year were not made explanatory variables in our model for practical data reasons, whereas these two variables are known to be important risk factors for default events. Having a pool-specific, non-time

---

[16] Macro variable, quarter: SPNAGDPY Index year on year Spanish GDP change.

[17] Macro variable, quarter: SPUNEMPR Index, Spain unemployment rate, in level.

[18] Macro variable, quarter: from SPUNEMPR Index, Spain unemployment rate, expressed in percentage change.

[19] Survey data variable, change in Consumer confidence, EUCCES Index.

[20] Survey data variable, change in Business confidence, SPHBINDX.

varying risk factor estimated from the data is a way to compensate for the lack of these two risk factors as well as potential other factors specific to a given pool and constant over time. We assume that the pool-specific factor follows a Gamma distribution of mean 1 and variance parameter theta, as commonly done in the literature. Theta is estimated by means of an EM algorithm[21]. Notice in passing that because this EM algorithm is needed to estimate the frailty theta, frailty models estimations are much more computer-intensive, in particular when using large databases such as the loan-level data.

Selection of the variables for the final model

We estimate a Cox proportional hazard rate model with shared frailty based on all pre-selected variables from loan-level data and with time-varying covariates from Bloomberg, then check the statistical significance of each variable. The sign of all the statistically significant coefficients makes sense with the exception of the unemployment rate change, which has an effect opposite to what expected: an increase of +1% in the change of unemployment rate, which means a higher unemployment rate, will result in a +6% decrease of the hazard rate. It has also a lower Wald statistic that all the other macroeconomic variables. We thus decide to exclude it from the final model. Business confidence, although significant, has a lower Wald statistic than unemployment rate change. For consistency with our choice of excluding unemployment, we exclude this variable too. Another argument for excluding this index is that it is somehow redundant with consumer confidence, which shows a higher statistical significance.

4.2.4 Final model

The estimates for our final model are reported below:

Breslow method for ties Number of obs = 337263
Gamma shared frailty Number of groups = 56; Group variable: ISIN
No. of subjects = 337263 Obs per group: min = 9
No. of failures = 20185 avg = 6022.554

---

[21] The first step of the EM algorithm is the estimation step E, whereby theta is kept unknown and an estimated frailty is computed as a function of theta. The maximum likelihood step M consists of refitting the model with the same covariates but including theta, for each possible value of theta (a discrete subset of possible values is chosen), and computing the maximum likelihood for each. The theta selected is the value of theta which maximises this likelihood.

4.2. COX-MODELLING OF DEFAULT RATES

Wald chi2(15) = 56320.14
Log likelihood = -206501.51 Prob > chi2 = 0.0000

variable	haz. ratio	std. err	Wald. z	P>|z|	95%. Conf. Interval
Legal form group (B)	0.57	0.11	−28.73	0	0.54-0.59
Borrower type group (B)	0.94	0.45	-1.28	0.2	0.85-1.03
Borrower type group (C)	0.86	0.33	-3.79	0	0.80-0.93
Borrower type group (D)	0.90	0.34	-2.75	0	0.83-0.97
Purpose group (B)	0.74	0.36	-5.93	0	0.67-0.82
Purpose group (C)	2.23	0.89	19.59	0	2.06-2.42
Purpose group (D)	1.61	0.43	17.66	0	1.52-1.70
Purpose group (E)	1.31	0.28	12.32	0	1.25-1.36
flotXInterestMarginMy	1.36	0.01	54.49	0	1.34-1.37
fixXInterestMarginMy	1.32	0.01	53.33	0	1.30-1.32
Collateral type (B)	1.26	0.03	10.23	0	1.20-1.31
Gross Domestic Product	0.52	0.00	-71.44	0	0.51-0.53
Consummer confidence	0.94	0.00	-60.98	0	0.94-0.94

Theta | .4190259 .0759239
Likelihood-ratio test of theta=0: chibar2(01) = 7668.53 Prob>=chibar2 = 0.000
Note: standard errors of hazard ratios are conditional on theta.

Loan-level data variables such as interest rate margin, legal form and loan purpose, all have a statistical significance comparable to macro-variables. It is a striking and very positive fact to find loan-level data fields that have a level of statistical significance (see the z-statistic) comparable to those of broad macroeconomic variables. Borrower type and collateral type have both a lower statistical significance.

We perform robustness tests on the coefficient by estimating different models with less variables and looking at the potential changes of the coefficients of the variable present in both models[22] and find that our coefficients are robust.

4.2.5 Model interpretation and consequences for risk assessment

In this section, we explain how to interpret each of the model parameter estimates. Because the precision and the reliability of these estimates ultimately depends on the quality of the loan level data, these interpretations should

---
[22] Results available from the author upon request.

be taken with caution. The Cox-modelling approach allows us to state the following results:

- compared to companies of legal form "Public Company", "Limited Company" or "Partnership", companies of legal form "Individual" or "others" or NA default 43% less often (and hence are almost twice less risky), all other factors being the same. This result happens to be very country-specific: in other jurisdictions the riskier legal forms will often be different ones;
- the Borrower Basel 3 Segment explanatory variable is also significant. Compared to "Corporates", "SMEs treated as Corporates" default at about the same rate, only 6% less quickly, which is small (recall PDs are already "low" numbers and the 6% decrease estimated is *relative to the PD of the baseline*). As such this result should not be over-interpreted and one could safely say that in Spain, "Corporates" or "SME treated as Corporates" have the same default rate, everything else being equal (for similar types of other characteristics). More interesting are the two other types, compared to the baseline: a Borrower Basel 3 Segment that is "Retail" entails a 14% lower hazard rate, while "Other" entails a 10 % lower hazard rate, everything else being equal;
- the Purpose of the loan is a very important risk factor. Compared to loans whose purpose is "Purchase", the two groups "Investment Mortgages" or "reinvestment" happen to have a 26% lower hazard rate. "Others, construction and real estate" default 31% quicker, "Working capital" and "no data" 61% quicker, and "Debt consolidation" is the riskier category of all, with defaults having a 123% higher probability of default than in the baseline of "Purchase";
- for floating interest loans, any increase of 1% of the spread above the index (EURIBOR, etc.) translates into a very significant +36% increase of the hazard rate;
- for fixed rate loans a 1% increase of the interest rate margin above the zero-coupon curve of its 10 year government bond translates itself into a similar significant increase of the rate of defaults of 31%;
- Collateral type which is not residential properties increases the hazard rate by 26%;
- an (instantaneous) increase of +1% of GDP translates itself into a 48% decrease of the default rate;
- an (instantaneous) increase of one point in the consumer confidence index translates into a negligible 6% decrease of the default rate.

Chapter 5

Conclusion

In this book we first reviewed the most widely used models of defaults, and explained them using an unified framework with consistent concepts and notations. These models often rely on some creditworthiness indicators which have to exceed some threshold for the loan to default, and on correlation coefficients which reflect common shocks to all the creditworthiness indicators of the loans within the pool.

We then presented two alternative, less well-known, ways to model default: Hidden Markov Chain models, which is a technique borrowed from the speech recognition literature, and Cox proportional hazard rate models, which are borrowed from the statistical field called Survival Analysis used in the testing of drugs and medical treatments. When modelling loans default through Hidden Markov Chains, correlation between defaults is induced by the common state of the credit cycle, which impacts all loans, and thus the approach shares some similarity with the more well-known Vasicek one-factor model approach. Empirical evidence in the European corporate bond market and the Spanish CLOs market suggested that default series clearly exhibit multi-state properties, which could support the use of multi-state Markov model to get more precise estimate of the probability of defaults in each state. Survival Analysis tools, because they can be used in a semi-parametric approach which estimates relative risks of individual loans depending on their characteristics, and not the baseline case itself, can be used on the loan-level data from the European DataWarehouse to extract relative-risk assessments that quantify how much additional risk, in terms of default and delinquencies, a specific loan characteristic entails. Survival Analysis thus provides a useful complementary tool for the modelling of defaults.

Bibliography

[1] Albrecher, H., Ladoucette, S. A., Schoutens W., 2007, "A generic one-factor Lévy model for synthetic CDOs", Advances in Mathematical Finance, R.J. Elliott et als edt., Birkhaeuser

[2] Banachewicz, K., van der Vaart, A., Lucas, A., "Modeling portfolio defaults using hidden Markov models with covariates", Tinbergen Institute Discussion Paper, TI 2006-094/2

[3] Basel Committee on Banking Supervision, 2006, "International convergence of capital measurement and capital standards: a revised framework"

[4] Bindseil et al (task force of the Market Operations Committee), 2007, "The use of portfolio credit risk models in central banks", Occasional Paper Series 64

[5] Black, F., Scholes, M., 1973. "The pricing of options and corporate liabilities", Journal of Political Economy vol 81, issue 3, 637-654

[6] Black, F., Cox, J., C., 1976. "Valuing corporate securities: some effects of bond indenture provisions ", Journal of Finance 31, 351-367

[7] Bluhm C., Overbeck L., Wagner C., 2002, "An introduction to credit risk modeling", Chapman & Hall/CRC Financial mathematic series

[8] David R, Cox, 1972. "Regression Models and Life-Tables", Journal of the Royal Statistical Society, Series B 34 (2), 187–220

[9] Ching, W-K, Siu, T-K, Li, L., Li, T., Li W-K, 2007, "Modeling default data via an interactive hidden Markov model"

[10] Duffie, D. ; Lando, D., 2001, "Term structure of credit spreads with incomplete accounting information," Econometrica 69, 633-664

[11] Cariboni, J., Schoutens, W., 2009, "Lévy processes in credit risk", Wiley Finance

[12] CreditMetrics^{TM} –Technical Document

[13] Dobransky P., Schoutens W., 2008, "Generic Lévy one-factor models for the joint modelling of prepayment and default: modelling LCDX"

[14] Geske, R., 1977, "The valuation of corporate liabilities as compound options", Journal of Financial and Quantitative Analysis 7, 63-81

[15] Giampieri, G., Davis, M., Crowder, M., 2005, "Analysis of default data using hidden Markov Models", Quantitative Finance, vol 5, issue 1

[16] Franke, J., Hardle, W. K., Hafner C. M., 2004, Statistics of Financial Markets, second edition, Springer

[17] Giesecke, K., 2005, "Default and information", Working Paper, Cornell University.

[18] Gordy, M. B., 2002, "A risk-factor model fundation for the ratings-based bank capital rules"

[19] Hilberink, B.; Rogers, L. C. G., 2002, "Optimal capital structure and endogenous default," Finance and Stochastics 6, 237-263.

[20] Ericsson, J., Reneby, J., 2005, "Estimating structural bond pricing models", Journal of Business 78,707-736.

[21] T. R., Fleming, D. P. Harrington, 1991, "Counting Process and Survival Analysis", John Wiley & Sons, Inc. New York, chapter IV.

[22] Heidorn, T., Kahlert, D., 2010, "Implied correlations of iTraxx tranches during the financial crisis," Frankfurt School Working Paper 145

[23] Hibbeln M., 2010, "Risk management in credit portfolios", Physica-Verlag

[24] Hull, J. C., 2006, "Options, futures and other derivatives", Sixth edition, Pearson

[25] Jarrow, R. A.; Protter, P., 2004, "Structural versus reduced form models: a new information based perspective," Journal of Investment Management 2, 1-10

[26] Kyprianou, E. A., 2006, "Introductory lectures on fluctuations of Lévy processes with applications", Springer

[27] Li, D. X.,1999, "On default correlation: a copula function approach," Working Paper 99-07, The Risk Metrics Group

[28] Merton, R., 1974, "On the Pricing of Corporate Debt: the Risk Structure of Interest Rates," Journal of Finance 29, 449-470

[29] Moody's, "Methodology for forecasting and stress-testing ABS and RMBS deals", Moody 'sAnalytics, 5 August 2010

[30] Moody's, "Moody's approach to real estate analysis for CMBS transactions in EMEA: portfolio analysis (MoRE Portfolio)"

[31] Moody's, "Update on Moody's approach to real estate analysis for CMBS transactions in EMEA"

[32] Nedeljkovic, J., Rosen, D., D Saunders, D. "Pricing and hedging collateralized loan obligations with implied factor models", The Journal of Credit Risk (53–97). vol 6, n. 3

[33] Rabiner L R, "A tutorial on hidden Markov models and selected applications in speech recognition", Proc. IEEE 77 257-286

[34] Schönbucher, P. J., and Schubert, D., 2001, "Copula-Dependent Default Risk in Intensity Models," Working Paper, Department of Statistics, Bonn University

[35] Vasicek, O. A., 2002, "The distribution of loan portfolio values", Risk

[36] Vasicek, O. A., 1997, "The loan loss distribution", Technical Report, KMV Corporation

[37] Zhou, C., 1997, "A jump-diffusion approach to modelling credit risk and valuing defaultable securities", Federal Reserve Board, Washington

BIBLIOGRAPHY

Chapter 6

Annex 1: formal proofs, derivations

6.1 Proof of the intensity model formula when $PD_i(t)$ is derivable

By definition, the instantaneous hazard rate $\lambda_{i,t}$ is the average probability of default of the loan i in over a very short time interval $[t, t+dt]$, knowing the loan has not defaulted before time t, hence we have:

$$\begin{aligned}
\lambda_{i,t} &= \lim_{dt \to 0} \left(\frac{P(t < \tau_i \leq t+dt \mid t > \tau_i)}{dt} \right) = \lim_{dt \to 0} \left(\frac{P(t < \tau_i \leq t+dt)}{P(t > \tau_i).dt} \right) \\
&= \lim_{dt \to 0} \left(\frac{PD_i(t+dt) - PD_i(t)}{(1 - PD_i(t)).dt} \right) \\
&= \frac{1}{1 - PD_i(t)} \lim_{dt \to 0} \left(\frac{PD_i(t+dt) - PD_i(t)}{dt} \right) \\
&= \frac{PD_i'(t)}{1 - PD_i(t)} = -\left(\frac{-PD_i'(t)}{1 - PD_i(t)} \right)
\end{aligned}$$

Hence $\lambda_{i,t}$ is integrable and integrating both sides yields:

$$\int_0^t \lambda_{i,s} ds = -\ln(1 - PD_i(t)) + \ln(1 - PD_i(0))$$

From which we deduce the expression of $PD_i(t)$ as a function of the trajectory $(\lambda_{i,t})_t$:

$$PD_i(t) := P(\tau_i \leq t) = 1 - \exp\left(-\int_0^t \lambda_{i,s} ds \right)$$

6.2 Merton threshold derivation

Merton assumes the value process $A_{i,t}$ of firm i is driven by:

$$dA_{i,t} = r_i A_{i,t} dt + \sigma_i A_{i,t} dW_{i,t}$$

Using Ito's lemma to find the dynamics of $d\ln(A_{i,T})$ and integrating one can derive the process driving $\ln(A_{i,t})$:

$$\ln(A_{i,T}) = \ln(A_{i,0}) + rT - \frac{\sigma_i^2}{2}T + \sigma_i \sqrt{T} Y_i$$

where Y_i is a standard normal gaussian variable.
Now, Merton assumes default if, and only if, the value of the firm falls below its debt level, idem est $A_{i,T} < B_{i,T}$. This is successively equivalent to

$$\ln(A_{i,T}) < \ln(B_{i,T})$$

$$\ln(A_{i,0}) + r_i T - \frac{\sigma_i^2}{2}T + \sigma_i \sqrt{T} Y_i < \ln(B_{i,T})$$

$$Y_i < \frac{\ln(B_{i,T}) - \ln(A_{i,0}) - r_i T + \frac{\sigma_i^2}{2}T}{\sigma_i \sqrt{T}}$$

Hence we can define:

$$c_i = \frac{\ln(B_{i,T}) - \ln(A_{i,0}) - r_i T + \frac{\sigma_i^2}{2}T}{\sigma_i \sqrt{T}}$$

6.3 CreditMetrics as a Merton model of default

CreditMetrics is based on the Merton model, although it does not model c_i explicitly. Indeed, the parameter c_i is not derived from Merton model, but calibrated using the corresponding empirical probability of default over the time horizon T, that is, $PD_i(T)$. Indeed from $\Phi(c_i) = PD_i(T)$ it follows that $c_i = \Phi^{-1}(PD_i(T))$.
Because by definition (see Annex 6.2)

$$\ln(A_{i,0}) + r_i T - \frac{\sigma_i^2}{2}T + \sigma_i \sqrt{T} Y_i = \ln(A_{i,T})$$

we have:

$$Y_i = \frac{\ln(A_{i,T}/A_{i,0}) - r_i T + \frac{\sigma_i^2}{2}T}{\sigma_i \sqrt{T}}$$

6.4. FROM MERTON TO VASICEK

Because under the Merton model Y_i is assumed to follow a standard normal distribution, the asset-value $\ln(A_{i,T}/A_{i,0})$, under the Merton model, has to follow a normal distribution of mean $r_i T - \frac{\sigma_i^2}{2}T$ and standard deviation $\sigma_i \sqrt{T}$.

CreditMetrics maps each borrower i to a country and a sector stock index. Then it uses this stock index as a proxy for the (unobservable) asset value process $A_{i,t}$. The obtained variable $\ln(A_{i,t}/A_{i,0})$ is then standardised, which as explained above results, under the assumptions of the Merton model, in a standard normal variable Y_i. This is the reason why in the CreditMetrics context Y_i is sometimes referred to as the *standardised log-return level*.

Then CreditMetrics decomposes Y_i as $Y_i = R_i \Psi_i + \epsilon_i$ where the ϵ_i are independent, identically distributed standard Gaussians and R_i is a Gaussian vector representing a systematic risk-factor independent from the ϵ_i, and Ψ_i is the corresponding vector of factor loadings, that is, the weight given to each risk factor in the model.

In Merton model default occurs if, and only if, $Y_i < c_i$, that is, if and only if $\epsilon_i < c_i - R_i \Psi_i$. Hence CreditMetrics obtains the probability of default conditional to the realisation of X as $P(\epsilon_i < c_i - R_i \Psi_i) = \Phi(c_i - R_i \Psi_i)$.

6.4 From Merton to Vasicek

Because Merton model is a model for a single firm, it makes no assumption on the cross-correlation of the Y_i derived above (Annex 6.2). Vasicek model consists simply in assuming that the Y_i can be written as

$$Y_i = \sqrt{\rho} Z + (\sqrt{1-\rho})\epsilon_i$$

where Z and the ϵ_i are mutually independent, identically distributed random variables following a standard normal law. Note that, by independence, the Y_i are themselves Gaussian, of variance 1 and expected value 0.

6.5 Vasicek derivation of pool default rate distribution for large homogenous portfolios

Let $p_i(Z)$ be the probability of default of loan i conditional to a realisation of the common factor Z. Then

$$\begin{aligned} p_i(Z) &= P(Y_i < c_i \,|\, Z) = P(\sqrt{\rho}Z + (\sqrt{1-\rho})\epsilon_i < c_i \,|\, Z) \\ &= P(\epsilon_i < \frac{c_i - \sqrt{\rho}Z}{\sqrt{1-\rho}}) \\ &= \Phi(\frac{c_i - \sqrt{\rho}Z}{\sqrt{1-\rho}}) \end{aligned}$$

Remark: Very often, this result is used to generalize the Vasicek one-factor model by letting Z follow any distribution (possibly not the standard normal Gaussian distribution).

The aim of the Vasicek model is to derive the default distribution of a given pool or porfolio of loans. To reach this aim it proceeds to make a certain number of assumptions. First, all the loans have equal size, and same probability of default $PD_i =: PD$. This implies $c_i = \Phi^{-1}(PD_i) = \Phi^{-1}(PD) =: c$. Second, the limiting distribution of losses is computed when n tends to infinity, meaning in practice that a high number of loans is required to apply the Vasicek model.

Let L_i be the default indicator of the ith loan, that is, L_i is the random variable equal to 1 if loan i defaults and 0 otherwise. Let $L = \frac{1}{n}\sum_i L_i$ be the pool default ratio. The core of Vasicek proof consists in noticing that since $P(L_i = 1 \,|\, Z) = P(Y_i < \Phi^{-1}(PD) \,|\, Z) = \Phi(\frac{\Phi^{-1}(PD) - \sqrt{\rho}Z}{\sqrt{1-\rho}})$, in the model the variable L_i are independently distributed when conditioned to the value of the common risk-factor Z. Hence, by the Law of Large Numbers, the arithmetic average $L = \frac{1}{n}\sum_i L_i$ converges to the distribution of L_i when n tends to infinity. Hence

$$P(L \leq x) = P(p_i(Z) \leq x) = P(Z \geq p_i^{-1}(x)) = \Phi(-p_i^{-1}(x))$$

since $p_i(x) = \Phi(\frac{c_i - \sqrt{\rho}x}{\sqrt{1-\rho}})$ is a decreasing function of x and Z is assumed to be a standard Gaussian law. Since

$$\begin{aligned} x &= p_i(y) \Leftrightarrow x = \Phi(\frac{c_i - \sqrt{\rho}y}{\sqrt{1-\rho}}) \\ &\Leftrightarrow \frac{c - \sqrt{1-\rho}\Phi^{-1}(x)}{\sqrt{\rho}} = y = p_i^{-1}(x) \end{aligned}$$

we have

$$P(L \leq x) = \Phi(\frac{\sqrt{1-\rho}\Phi^{-1}(x) - c}{\sqrt{\rho}})$$
$$= \Phi(\frac{\sqrt{1-\rho}\Phi^{-1}(x) - \Phi^{-1}(PD)}{\sqrt{\rho}})$$

6.6 VaR and ES in Gordy and Vasicek framework

Two main results from Gordy's framework [18] are the derivation of the VaR(α) and of the $ES(\alpha)$ for the limiting loss distribution of a portfolio whose Herfindahl index tends to 0, assuming a single factor is able to capture all the co-dependence between loans in the portfolio. In the examples of the use of that framework chosen in this book (Basel II capital requirements), losses *after recovery* are taken into account. Hence this section makes an exception compared to the rest of the book and explicitly considers recoveries values. Let LGD_i be the loss given default of loan i. Hence a total monetary loss following default corresponds to the special case where $LGD_i = 100\%$. Let D_i be the event of default of loan i. Hence, if the time-frame of our one-period model is $[0, T]$, the event D_i is linked to the previously defined random variables τ_i and L_i by:

$$D_i = (\tau_i \leq T) = (L_i = 1)$$

The VaR of the limiting loss distribution is then:

$$\text{VaR}(\alpha) = E(\sum_i w_i LGD_i 1_{D_i} \mid Z = \Phi^{-1}(1-\alpha))$$

This result is admitted here[1]. Crucial to Gordy's derivation is that the default events once conditioned on the realisation of the common factor Z are independent. Assuming the exposures of each individual loan w_i are fixed and that each LGD_i is, conditionally to Z, independent from the default event D_i, we can write:

$$\text{VaR}(\alpha) = \sum_i w_i E(LGD_i \mid Z = \Phi^{-1}(1-\alpha)) E(1_{D_i} \mid Z = \Phi^{-1}(1-\alpha))$$

Now the expression $E(1_{D_i} \mid Z = \Phi^{-1}(1-\alpha)) = E(1_{D_i} \mid Z = -\Phi^{-1}(\alpha)) = P(L_i = 1 \mid Z = -\Phi^{-1}(\alpha))$ is the probability of default of loan i subject to a

---

[1] The above formula also holds for Z following a different distribution than a standard gaussian one: just replace Φ^{-1} by F_Z^{-1}. A proof, in the general setting, can be found in [23], Annex 2.8.9, page 53, or in Gordy original article [18].

given value $(-\Phi^{-1}(\alpha))$ of the risk factor Z. It is thus a known expression in the Vasicek framework (see Annex 6.5):

$$E(1_{D_i} | Z = -\Phi^{-1}(\alpha)) = \Phi(\frac{c_i - \sqrt{\rho_i}x}{\sqrt{1-\rho_i}})$$

with $c_i = \Phi^{-1}(PD_i)$ and $x = -\Phi^{-1}(\alpha)$ and where ρ_i corresponds to the correlation within the assets of a (imaginary) pool made of loans similar to loan i. This probability of default conditional to a systemic factor event is then plugged into Gordy's formula:

$$\text{VaR}(\alpha) = \sum_i w_i E(LGD_i | Z = \Phi^{-1}(1-\alpha))\Phi(\frac{\Phi^{-1}(PD_i) + \sqrt{\rho_i}\Phi^{-1}(\alpha)}{\sqrt{1-\rho_i}})$$

The ES of the limiting loss distribution can be expressed as[2]

$$ES(\alpha) = \frac{1}{1-\alpha} \int_\alpha^1 \text{VaR}(u) du$$

Using the previous formula for expressing VaR(u), and assuming a fixed value for the stressed (conditional) expected loss given defaut $E(LGD_i | Z = \Phi^{-1}(1-\alpha)) =: ELGD_i^{stressed}$ yields:

$$ES(\alpha) = \frac{1}{1-\alpha} \int_\alpha^1 \sum_i w_i ELGD_i^{stressed} \Phi(\frac{\Phi^{-1}(PD_i) + \sqrt{\rho_i}\Phi^{-1}(u)}{\sqrt{1-\rho_i}}) du$$

$$= \frac{1}{1-\alpha} \sum_i w_i ELGD_i^{stressed} \int_\alpha^1 \Phi(\frac{\Phi^{-1}(PD_i) + \sqrt{\rho_i}\Phi^{-1}(u)}{\sqrt{1-\rho_i}}) du$$

But the change of variable $u = \Phi(-x)$ gives, since $\phi(-x) = \phi(x)$:

$$\int_\alpha^1 \Phi(\frac{\Phi^{-1}(PD_i) + \sqrt{\rho}\Phi^{-1}(u)}{\sqrt{1-\rho}}) du = -\int_{-\Phi^{-1}(\alpha)}^{-\Phi^{-1}(1)} \Phi(\frac{\Phi^{-1}(PD_i) - \sqrt{\rho_i}x}{\sqrt{1-\rho_i}})\phi(-x)dx$$

$$= -\int_{-\Phi^{-1}(\alpha)}^{-\infty} \Phi(\frac{\Phi^{-1}(PD_i) - \sqrt{\rho_i}x}{\sqrt{1-\rho_i}})\phi(x)dx$$

$$= \int_{-\infty}^{-\Phi^{-1}(\alpha)} \Phi(\frac{\Phi^{-1}(PD_i) - \sqrt{\rho_i}x}{\sqrt{1-\rho_i}})\phi(x)dx$$

$$= \Phi_2(-\Phi^{-1}(\alpha), \Phi^{-1}(PD_i), \sqrt{\rho_i})$$

where we used that

$$\Phi_2(x, z, a) = \int_{-\infty}^z \Phi(\frac{x - ay}{\sqrt{1-a^2}})\phi(y)dy$$

---

[2] This general fact is admitted here. For a proof the reader can refer to Acerbi and Tasche (2002), "On the cooherence of expected shortfall" J Bank Fin 26 (7), page 1492.

Hence

$$ES(\alpha) = \frac{1}{1-\alpha} \sum_i w_i ELGD_i^{stressed} \Phi_2(-\Phi^{-1}(\alpha), \Phi^{-1}(PD_i), \sqrt{\rho_i})$$

6.7 Simulating the reduced Gaussian copula model

Here we study a particular case of Gaussian copula, show how simulations of this reduced Gaussian copula model can easily be obtained, and how it is consistent with the structural one-factor Vasicek model. We also explain in detail how to simulate time to default within this framework.

Let $C(u_1, ..., u_k) := P(F_1(Y_1) \leq u_1, ..., F_1(Y_1) \leq u_k)$ be a Gaussian copula; it is associated to a Gaussian cdf $F_{(Y_1,...Y_k)} = F$. Without loss of generality, we can assume the Y_i are standard normal variables. We seek to impose the following simple linear correlation structure: the images of marginal $F_i^{-1}(U_i) = Y_i$ of the copula C have to satisfy:

$$Corr(Y_i, Y_j) =: \rho \text{ for all } i \neq j$$

The coefficient ρ is often called "asset correlation", because asset price correlations are often used as a proxy for ρ. It is thus a parameter of the copula, which has been reduced in its generality by assuming only a *single* cross-asset correlation, instead of the general $n(n-1)/2$ possibly distinct cross-correlations. This simplifying assumption is often made in default modelling.

A way to obtain the condition $Corr(Y_i, Y_j) =: \rho$ for all $i \neq j$, is to simulate $k+1$ independent and identically distributed random variables $U'_1, ..., U'_{k+1}$ and then compute $Y_i = \sqrt{1-\rho}\Phi^{-1}(U'_i) + \sqrt{\rho}\Phi^{-1}(U'_{k+1})$, where Φ is the cdf of a standard normal Gaussian.

Indeed, by bilinearity of the covariance and by independence we have:

$$Cov(Y_i, Y_j) = \rho Var(\Phi^{-1}(U'_{k+1})) = \rho \sqrt{Var(\Phi^{-1}(U'_i))} \sqrt{Var(\Phi^{-1}(U'_j))}$$

and, since by independence of the $\Phi^{-1}(U'_i)$ with the $\Phi^{-1}(U'_{k+1})$:

$$\begin{aligned} Var(Y_i) &= Var(\sqrt{1-\rho}\Phi^{-1}(U'_i) + \sqrt{\rho}\Phi^{-1}(U'_{k+1})) \\ &= (1-\rho)Var(\Phi^{-1}(U'_i)) + \rho Var(\Phi^{-1}(U'_{k+1})) \\ &= Var(\Phi^{-1}(U'_i)) \end{aligned}$$

we do get

$$Corr(Y_i, Y_j) = \frac{Cov(Y_i, Y_j)}{Var(Y_i)} = \frac{Cov(Y_i, Y_j)}{\sqrt{Var(Y_i)}\sqrt{Var(Y_j)}} = \rho$$

This derivation explains the choice of the form for the coefficients $\sqrt{1-\rho}$ and $\sqrt{\rho}$. It is important to note that the correlation coefficient ρ, which is indeed a Pearson-correlation coefficient at the level of the random variables $Y_i = \Phi^{-1}(U_i) = \Phi^{-1}(PD_i(\tau_i))$, is not necessarily the Pearson correlation coefficient for the final variables explained (the τ_i), nor the "uniformalized" ones (the $U_i = PD_i(\tau_i)$). Note that in the case of a Gaussian copula, because the cross-correlation between a standard multivariate Gaussian vector determine entirely the distribution, the assumption that $Corr(Y_i, Y_j) = \rho$ for all i, j entirely characterizes the distribution.

Now, notice that we wrote:

$$Y_i = \sqrt{1-\rho}\,\Phi^{-1}(U_i') + \sqrt{\rho}\,\Phi^{-1}(U_{k+1}')$$

Letting $\epsilon_i := \Phi^{-1}(U_i')$ and $Z := \Phi^{-1}(U_{k+1}')$ this is

$$Y_i = \sqrt{\rho}\,Z + (\sqrt{1-\rho})\epsilon_i$$

ϵ_i is called the idiosyncratic factor associated to loan i while Z is called the systematic risk factor, as it is common to all Y_i. Hence simulating random variables for the purpose of using the (statistical) copula model yields a structural model, in which Y_i, which can be interpreted as the credit-quality of loan i, is influenced both by an idiosyncratic factor ϵ_i and a systematic factor Z which affects all the loans of the portfolio. Because ϵ_i and Z are normally distributed by Lemma 1, this is precisely the *Vasicek one-factor model*. Notice that by independence of Z and ϵ_i, the two-dimensional random vectors (Z, ϵ_i) are Gaussians, and hence as a linear combination of them the variable Y_i is also Gaussian. This is the reason why the resulting model is sometimes called the *standard single-factor Gaussian copula model*.

The simulated default time t_i (realisation of the variable τ_i) is the time which solves:

$$PD_i(t_i) = u_i$$

where u_i is a realisation of $U_i = \Phi(Y_i)$. This solves into

$$1 - \exp(-t_i \lambda_i) = u_i$$
$$t_i = \frac{\ln(1-u_i)}{-\lambda_i}$$

Chapter 7

Annex 2: Hidden Markov Chains

7.1 Efficient algorithms

7.1.1 Expressing the likelihood

The practical strength of hidden Markov chains (HMMs) is that there exists an efficient algorithm to compute the likelihood of the model being in a given state knowing the observation sequence. We describe below in a succinct but self-contained way the main results that served as a basis to implement HMMs for default series.

Let N be the number of hidden states of the underlying Markov model. Without loss of generality we can label these states from 1 to N. For illustration purposes we only considered two states: a low risk state, and a high risk state, hence $N = 2$, but the results and algorithms presented in this section can apply to an arbitrary number of states N. Let T be the length of the sample of observations. Without loss of generality, time is labelled from 1 to T. Let $A = (a_{ij})_{i,j}$ be the state-transition probability matrix of the model time-invariant hidden Markov chain; it is defined by:

$$a_{ij} = P(S_{t+1} = j \mid S_t = i)$$

For each state i in $\{1, 2, ..., N\}$, the number of defaults at time t, assuming the underlying state is i, is the realisation of a random variable which follows a discrete probability distribution function $B_t(i)$ (or, in the continuous-observation case, a probability distribution of *density* $B_t(i)$) supported by $\{1, 2, ..., n_t\}$ (in the discrete case) where n_t is the size of the sample at time t. For k in

$\{1, 2, ..., n_t\}$ we denote by $B_t(i)(k)$ the probability of observing the value k under $B_t(i)$ (or, in the continuous-observation case, the density of k under $B_t(i)$).

Let $\pi = (\pi_1, \pi_2)$ be the initial distribution, and let $\lambda = (A, B, \pi)$ be the model. Let $S = S_1...S_T$ be the underlying sequence of states of the HMM. Let $O = O_1...O_T$ be the sequence of observations. Hence, O_t is the realisation of a random variable of law $B_t(S_t)$ and belongs to $\{1, 2, ..., n_t\}$. Using basic properties of Markov chains and the model definition it is clear that the probability $P(O, S)$ of observing the sequence O while having the underlying state sequence S is simply:

$$P(O, S) = \pi_{S_1} a_{S_1 S_2} B_1(S_1)(O_1) a_{S_2 S_3} B_2(S_2)(O_2)...a_{S_{T-1} S_T} B_T(S_T)(O_T)$$

Re-grouping similar terms yields:

$$P(O, S) = \pi_{S_1} \prod_{t=1}^{T-1} a_{S_t S_{t+1}} \prod_{t=1}^{T} B_t(S_t)(O_t)$$

Hence the log-likelihood can be written as:

$$\log(P(O, S)) = \log(\pi_{S_1}) + \sum_{t=1}^{T-1} \log(a_{S_t S_{t+1}}) + \sum_{t=1}^{T} \log(B_t(S_t)(O_t))$$

At this point it is convenient to introduce the following indicator functions $\gamma_t(i)$, for t in $\{1, 2, ..., T\}$, and $\gamma_t(i, j)$, for t in $\{1, 2, ..., T-1\}$, which are dependent on the random variables S_t, and defined by:

$$\gamma_t(i) = 1_{(S_t = i)} = \begin{cases} 1 \text{ if } S_t = i \\ 0 \text{ otherwise} \end{cases}$$

and

$$\gamma_t(i, j) = 1_{(S_t = i, S_{t+1} = j)} = \begin{cases} 1 \text{ if } S_t = i \text{ and } S_{t+1} = j \\ 0 \text{ otherwise} \end{cases}$$

The log-likelihood can be re-written as (notice the re-writting only consists in adding terms of zero values):

$$\log(P(O, S)) = \sum_{i=1}^{N} \gamma_1(i) \log(\pi_i) + \sum_{i=1}^{N} \sum_{j=1}^{N} \sum_{t=1}^{T-1} \gamma_t(i, j) \log(a_{ij}) +$$
$$\sum_{i=1}^{N} \sum_{t=1}^{T} \gamma_t(i) \log(B_t(i)(O_t))$$

The algorithm consists in repeating a certain number of times the following two steps.

7.1. EFFICIENT ALGORITHMS

First, compute estimates $\widehat{\gamma_t(i)}$ and $\widehat{\gamma_t(i,j)}$ of the parameters $\gamma_t(i)$ and $\gamma_t(i,j)$, knowing $O = O_1...O_T$ and assuming the current values of the model (A, B, π). To this aim use efficient algorithms based on the recursive relations described below for computation, but rescal at each step to avoid underflow. These estimates $\widehat{\gamma_t(i)}$ and $\widehat{\gamma_t(i,j)}$ replace, in the expression above, the true values $\gamma_t(i)$ and $\gamma_t(i,j)$.

Second, each term of the resulting maximum likelihood estimate is maximised with respect to the model parameters (A, B, π) separately. This is possible because π only appears in the first term, A in the second and B_t in the third. Moreover, notice that in the second term the $\sum_{j=1}^{N} \sum_{t=1}^{T-1} \gamma_t(i,j) \log(a_{ij})$ can be maximised independently (subject to the linear constraint $\sum_{j=1}^{N} a_{ij} = 1$), and that similarly the third term is made of the N separate sums

$$\sum_{t=1}^{T-1} \gamma_t(i) \log(B_t(i)(O_t))$$

which can be maximised separately.

7.1.2 The first step

In what follows we detail efficient algorithms for computing the estimates of $\gamma_t(i)$ and $\gamma_t(i,j)$. For simplicity of notation, we will drop the hat, hence $\gamma_t(i)$ and $\gamma_t(i,j)$ stand for $\widehat{\gamma_t(i)}$ and $\widehat{\gamma_t(i,j)}$.
By definition,

$$\gamma_t(i) = P(S_t = i \mid O, \lambda) = \frac{P(S_t = i, O \mid \lambda)}{P(O \mid \lambda)}$$

$$\gamma_t(i,j) = P(S_t = i, S_{t+1} = j \mid O, \lambda) = \frac{P(S_t = i, S_{t+1} = j, O \mid \lambda)}{P(O \mid \lambda)}$$

To compute $P(S_t = i, O \mid \lambda)$ efficiently, as well as $P(O \mid \lambda)$, we introduce the so-called "forward paths". Let i be in $\{1, ..., N\}$ and t be in $\{1, ..., T\}$. We define the forward path $\alpha_t(i)$ as:

$$\alpha_t(i) = P(S_t = i, O_1...O_t \mid \lambda)$$

Clearly
$$\alpha_1(i) = P(S_1 = i, O_1 \mid \lambda) = \pi_i . B_1(i)(O_1)$$

Then the others $\alpha_t(i)$, for t in $\{2, ..., T\}$ can be computed recursively by noticing that:

$$\alpha_t(i) = \sum_{j=1}^{N} \alpha_{t-1}(j) . a_{ji} . B_t(i)(O_t)$$

The recursive formula is obtained by simply noticing that the only way to end up in state i at time t, for t in $\{2, ..., T\}$, while producing the observation sequence $O_1...O_t$ is to have been in some prior state j at time $t-1$ and having produced $O_1...O_{t-1}$ (probability $\alpha_{t-1}(j)$) and moving from state j to state i in the next step (probability a_{ji}) while producing the observation O_t in state i at time t (probability $B_t(i)(O_t)$). Independence of these events implies the product $\alpha_{t-1}(j).a_{ji}.B_t(i)(O_t)$ of these probabilities is the probability of such an event.

There are many ways to express $P(O\,|\,\lambda)$ as a function of the other introduced quantities:

$$\begin{aligned} P(O\,|\,\lambda) &= \sum_{i=1}^{N} P(S_T = i, O_1...O_T\,|\,\lambda) = \sum_{i=1}^{N} \alpha_T(i) \\ &= \sum_{i=1}^{N}\sum_{j=1}^{N} P(S_t = i, S_{t+1} = j, O\,|\,\lambda) = \sum_{i=1}^{N}\sum_{j=1}^{N} \gamma_t(i,j) \text{ for every } t \end{aligned}$$

Hence computing the forward paths gives an efficient algorithm to obtain the likelihood of observing O given the model λ.

Let i be in $\{1, ..., N\}$ and t be in $\{1, ..., T\}$. We define the "backward paths" $\beta_t(i)$ as:

$$\beta_T(i) = 1 \text{ by convention, and:}$$

$$\beta_t(i) = P(S_t = i, O_{t+1}...O_T\,|\,\lambda)$$

They can be computed recursively in a similar fashion to the $\alpha_t(i)$, but "backward", meaning, starting from $t = T - 1$, as

$$\beta_t(i) = \sum_{j=1}^{N} a_{ij}.B_{t+1}(j)(O_{t+1}).\beta_{t+1}(j)$$

Indeed $\beta_t(i) = P(S_t = i, O_{t+1}...O_T\,|\,\lambda) = \sum_{j=1}^{N} a_{ij}.B_{t+1}(j)(O_{t+1}).P(S_{t+1} = j, O_{t+2}...O_T\,|\,\lambda)$.

Now, it follows trivially from the definition of $\alpha_t(i)$ and $\beta_t(i)$ that, for all t in $\{1, ..., T\}$ and all i in $\{1, ..., N\}$:

$$P(S_t = i, O\,|\,\lambda) = \alpha_t(i)\beta_t(i)$$

Hence the expression for $\gamma_t(i)$:

$$\gamma_t(i) = \frac{\alpha_t(i)\beta_t(i)}{P(O\,|\,\lambda)}$$

7.1. EFFICIENT ALGORITHMS

Similarly we can compute the $\gamma_t(i,j)$ from the $\alpha_t(i)$ and $\beta_t(i)$ as:

$$\begin{aligned}\gamma_t(i,j) &= P(S_t = i, S_{t+1} = j | O, \lambda) \\ &= \frac{P(S_t = i, S_{t+1} = j, O | \lambda)}{P(O|\lambda)} \\ &= \frac{\alpha_t(i).a_{ij}.B_{t+1}(j)(O_{t+1}).\beta_{t+1}(j)}{P(O|\lambda)}\end{aligned}$$

Also, notice that, for t in $\{1, ..., T-1\}$:

$$\gamma_t(i) = \sum_{j=1}^{N} \gamma_t(i,j)$$

This is the formula we used for computing $\gamma_t(i)$ from the $\gamma_t(i,j)$, with the exception of $t = T$.

The second step

We know turn our attention to the maximisation of the log-likelihood estimate obtained. As mentionned earlier, the three terms appearing in the sum can be maximised separately. To prove all the three results above is simply done by equating the partial derivatives to 0. We do not detail the computation, but the two first results can be found in the literature (see for example, [33]).

a) The first term, $\sum_{i=1}^{N} \gamma_1(i) \log(\pi_i)$, is maximised for $\pi_i = \gamma_1(i)$.

b) The second for $a_{ij} = \frac{f_{ij}}{\sum_{k=1}^{N} f_{ik}}$ where $f_{ij} := \sum_{t=1}^{T-1} \gamma_t(i,j)$.

c) The third term, as noticed above, can be split for the purpose of maximisation into N distinct maximisation problems. The value or set of values which realise the maximum depends, of course, of the form assumed for the probability distribution functions $B_t(i)$. In the case of a binomial distribution of parameter n_t and p_i, we get:

$$\sum_{t=1}^{T} \gamma_t(i) \log(B_t(i)(O_t)) = \sum_{t=1}^{T} \gamma_t(i)(\log(\binom{n_t}{O_t}) + O_t.\log(p_t) + (n_t - x_t).\log(1-p_t))$$

whose maximum is attained at:

$$p_i = \frac{\sum_{t=1}^{T} \gamma_t(i).O_t}{\sum_{t=1}^{T} \gamma_t(i).n_t}$$

Notice that O_t is the number of defaults at time t, hence the number above makes sense; in particular p_i belongs to $[0,1]$. In the particular case where $n_t =: n$ is constant (as assumed for example when dealing with rates) meaning that at each step it is assumed that the number of re-introduced loans compensates exactly for the previous step defaults, we get the somehow simpler formula: $p_i = \frac{1}{n} \frac{\sum_{t=1}^{T} \gamma_t(i).O_t}{\sum_{t=1}^{T} \gamma_t(i)}$.

7.1.3 Obtention of confidence interval through parametric bootstrap

Parametric bootstrapping simply consists in simulating with the fitted model $\hat{\Theta}$ a large number K of samples of the same size T and fitting each of the simulated sample to obtain parameter estimates $\widehat{\Theta_1}, \widehat{\Theta_2}, ..., \widehat{\Theta_K}$. The empirical distribution of these estimates $\widehat{\Theta_1}, \widehat{\Theta_2}, ..., \widehat{\Theta_K}$ then provides an indication about the model stability. In particular, an empirical variance-covariance matrix of all the model parameters can be computed in the usual way:

$$\widehat{Var}(\hat{\Theta}) = \frac{1}{K-1} \sum_{i=1}^{K} (\widehat{\Theta_i} - \overline{\hat{\Theta}})'.(\widehat{\Theta_i} - \overline{\hat{\Theta}})$$

where $\overline{\hat{\Theta}} := \frac{1}{K} \sum_{i=1}^{K} \widehat{\Theta_i}$ and $'$ denote the matrix transpose operator.

Notice that the initial guessed values for the estimate still have to be selected. As a rule, we decided to always select the same initial values than the one which led to the fitted model $\hat{\Theta}$.

7.1.4 Obtention of h step forward forecasts from the model

Assume we want to obtain the h step forward forecast from the HMM model λ at time t. As we observed $O_1...O_t$, the probability of observing O_{t+h} in h periods from now, where O_{t+h} is, in this section, any element of the observation set $\{1, 2, ..., n_t\}$, is simply the quantity

$$P(O_{t+h} | O_1...O_t, \lambda) = \frac{P(O_{t+h}, O_1...O_t | \lambda)}{P(O_1...O_t | \lambda)}$$

7.1. EFFICIENT ALGORITHMS

Clearly, $P(O_1...O_t | \lambda) = \sum_{k=1}^{N} \alpha_t(k)$. For the numerator now, using in a similar way the formula for total probabilities, we can write:

$$P(O_{t+h}, O_1...O_t | \lambda) = \sum_{i=1}^{N} P(O_{t+h}, S_t = i, O_1...O_t | \lambda)$$

$$= \sum_{i=1}^{N} \sum_{j=1}^{N} P(O_{t+h}, S_{t+h} = j, S_t = i, O_1...O_t | \lambda)$$

$$= \sum_{i=1}^{N} \sum_{j=1}^{N} \alpha_t(i).a_{ij}(h).B_{t+h}(j)(O_{t+h})$$

where $a_{ij}(h) := P(S_{t+h} = j | S_t = i)$ is simply the (i,j) th coefficient of the matrix A^h (easy to check). Hence:

$$P(O_{t+h} | O_1...O_t, \lambda) = \frac{\sum_{i=1}^{N} \sum_{j=1}^{N} \alpha_t(i).a_{ij}(h).B_{t+h}(j)(O_{t+h})}{\sum_{k=1}^{N} \alpha_t(k)}$$

$$= \sum_{i=1}^{N} \sum_{j=1}^{N} \tilde{\alpha}_t(i).a_{ij}(h).B_{t+h}(j)(O_{t+h})$$

where $\tilde{\alpha}_t(i) = \frac{\alpha_t(i)}{\sum_{k=1}^{N} \alpha_t(k)}$ are the rescaled forward paths.

In the case of one step forward forecasts for a two state HMM this becomes:

$$P(O_{t+1} | O_1...O_t, \lambda) = \tilde{\alpha}_t(1).a_{11}.B_{t+1}(j)(O_{t+1}) + \tilde{\alpha}_t(1).a_{12}.B_{t+1}(2)(O_{t+1}) +$$
$$\tilde{\alpha}_t(2).a_{21}.B_{t+1}(1)(O_{t+1}) + \tilde{\alpha}_t(2).a_{22}.B_{t+1}(2)(O_{t+1})$$

Remark: in case we would like to obtain *out-of-sample forecasts* from a HMM model, notice that these forward forecasts are not strictly speaking out-of-sample forecasts when the parameter estimates of the fitted model have taken into account the observations after time t.

7.1.5 Assessing the goodness-of-fit of the model through the forward mid-pseudo residuals

Let $\tilde{O}_{t+1}$ be the random variable indicating the number of defaults at time $t + 1$. Hence, its realisation is O_{t+1}. From the above we can compute the empirical cumulative distribution function of $\tilde{O}_{t+1}$ conditional on the model λ and on observing $O_1...O_t$: this is simply

$$P(\tilde{O}_{t+1} \leq x | O_1...O_t, \lambda) = \sum_{k \leq x} P(k | O_1...O_t, \lambda)$$

where $P(k|O_1...O_t, \lambda)$ can be computed from the formula given in Section 7.1.4.

The one-step ahead forward pseudo-residual at time t is then, by definition:

$$P(\tilde{O}_{t+1} \leq O_{t+1}|O_1...O_t, \lambda)$$

By applying Lemma 2 at each different time t, for t in $\{1, ..., T\}$, we get that these forward pseudo-residuals are all uniformely distributed. This provides a way to assess the goodness-of-fit of the model: if the data-generating process is indeed equal or close to the fitted model, we should observe that the forward pseudo-residuals follow closely a uniform distribution. This can be check visually using histogram and (uniform) quantile-to-quantile plot.

A drawback of the use of a uniform distribution is that it is difficult to determine outliers, as low or high values are repectively mapped close to 0 or 1. Hence we further transform these uniformly distributed quantiles into standard normal ones using Lemma 1: if Φ is the cdf of a standard normal law, then the

$$z_t = \Phi^{-1}(P(\tilde{O}_{t+1} \leq O_{t+1}|O_1...O_t, \lambda))$$

are realisations of a standard normal law.
Because the probability distribution of the number of default is discrete, we make a last adjustement by considering the average of the uniform upper and lower quantiles before applying Φ^{-1}. Hence, we get:

$$z_t = \Phi^{-1}(\frac{P(X < O_{t+1}|O_1...O_t, \lambda) + P(X \leq O_{t+1}|O_1...O_t, \lambda)}{2})$$

These are called (normal) mid-pseudo residuals, and normality tests can be performed directly on the z_t.

7.1.6 Non-homogeneous hidden Markov chains

Markov chains can be made dependent on covariates $X(t)$, which can result in non-stationary processes for the coefficients of the transition probability matrix A. The algorithms described in the previous sections are still valid when one
- replaces the a_{ij} by $a_{ij}(t)$, where $a_{ij}(t)$ is the (i, j) th coefficient of the transition probability matrix at time t, denoted by $A(t)$,

7.1. EFFICIENT ALGORITHMS

- specifies a dependence structure betwen $A(t)$ and the covariates $X(t)$. For example, the loggistic transformation with $X(t)$ representing a single covariate gives the model:

$$a_{ii}(t) = \frac{1}{\exp(X(t).\Psi_{ij} + \eta_{ij})}$$
$$a_{ij}(t) = 1 - a_{ii}(t) \text{ for } i \neq j$$

with Ψ_{ij} and η_{ij} parameters to estimate.
- replaces the second step of Section 7.1.2 by numerical maximisation, as no closed-formula is known.

7.1.7 An example with binomially-simulated data

The define the data-generating process has having the state-transition probability matrix:

$$A = \begin{bmatrix} 0.9 & 0.1 \\ 0.1 & 0.9 \end{bmatrix}$$

Hence, being in any state at a given period, there is a 90% probability to stay in the same state in the following period and a 10% probability to change state. We also set the individual loan probability of default at $p_1 = 0.004$ in the low risk state and at twice this number in the enhanced state: $p_2 = 0.008$. We simulate $T = 80$ observations with a sample of constant size $n = 1000$. The initial state is the low risk state (state 1), that is, we set the initial probability distribution to $\pi = (1, 0)$.
To start our estimation, we make the following (very rough) guess: $A_{guessed} = \begin{bmatrix} 0.5 & 0.5 \\ 0.5 & 0.5 \end{bmatrix}$, $\pi_{guessed} = (0.5, 0.5)$ and $p_{1,guessed} = 0.001$, $p_{2,guessed} = 0.020$. We allow for 100 iterations for maximising the log-likelihood as described in Annex 7.1.1, which results in the estimated parameter indicated, together with our starting guess and the true model parameters, in the table below[1]:

	initial guess	parameter estimates	true data-generating process
π_1	0.5	1	1
π_2	0.5	0	0
p_1	0.0001	0.0034	0.004
p_2	0.0020	0.0079	0.008
a_{11}	0.5	0.8823	0.9
a_{22}	0.5	0.9123	0.9

[1]To ensure reproducibility of results we used the Matlab command rng(5) to set the seed of the random number generator.

A state-sequence retrieval algorithm can then be applied to the fitted model to try to recover this true state sequence. The graph on the top left-hand corner of Figure 7.1 below indicates the default series generated and the underlying true state sequence. The other graphs indicate the retrieved state sequence, through either the Matlab built-in Viterbi algorithm, the author's own implementation of the Viterbi algorithm, or the author's HMM algorithm which maximises the *expected number of correct states*, as an alternative to maximising the likelihood of a given chain sequence among all possible state sequence as in the Viterbi algorithm.

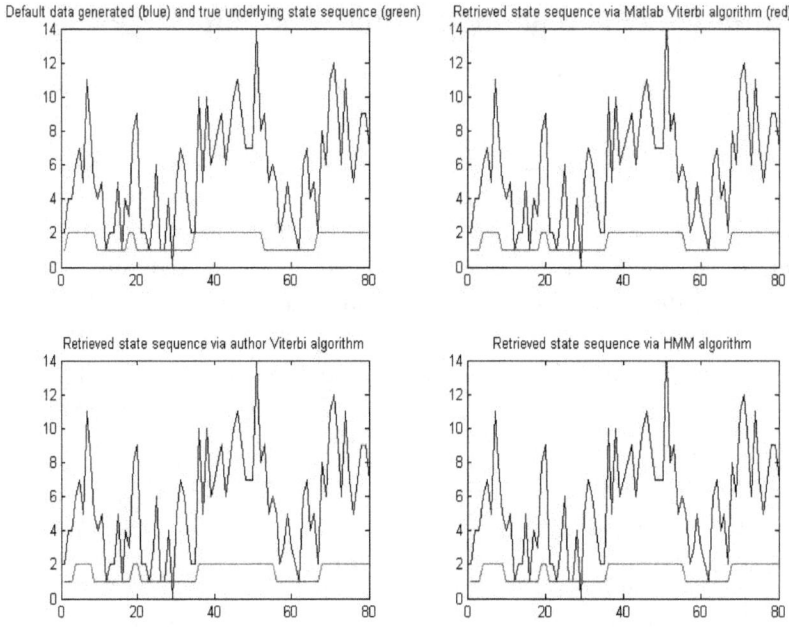

Figure 7.1: Simulated default data and state sequences (true one and retrieved)

Because we simulate the numerical example on which the calibration is applied, we know the true underlying state sequence. We can compute the Hamming distance between the true sequence and the retrieved one, and translate it into the score of the total number of correctly retrieved states divided by the total number of states (which is 80 in our example). The results for this particular simulation are reported below:

7.1. EFFICIENT ALGORITHMS

	author's Viterbi	Matlab Viterbi	author's HMM
score	0.8750	0.8750	0.8875

The goodness of fit of the model can be assessed through the computation of the so-called mid-pseudo residuals (see Annex 7.1.5). If the fitted model is correct, these residuals should be standard normal. Figure 7.2 below indicates, from top to bottom and left to right: the data series of the residuals of our simulation, their fit vis-a-vis of the standard Gaussian law via a histogram and a quantile-to-quantile plot, and their partial autocorrelation function (PACF). Notice in HMM models it is perfectly normal for residuals to be correlated: this does not have negative implications for the validity of the model.

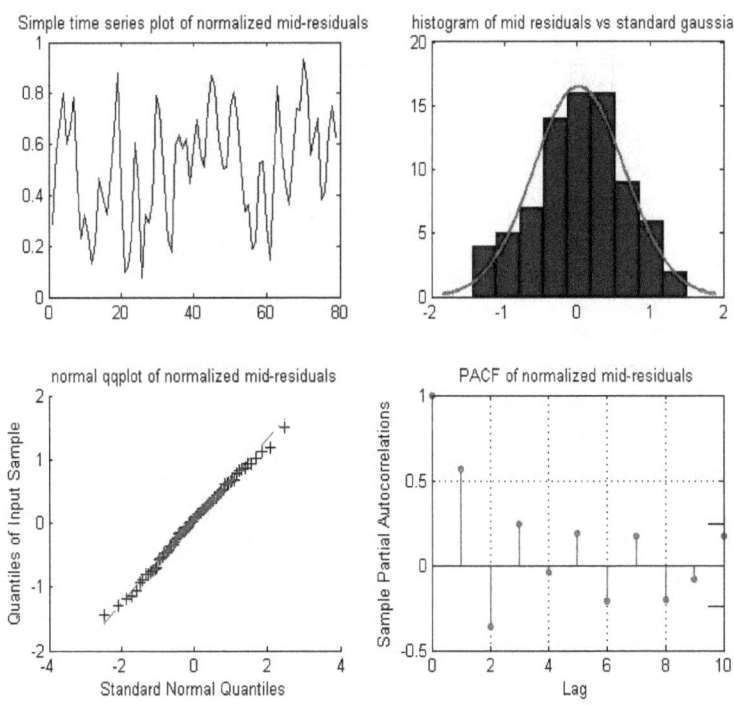

Figure 7.2: Analysis of the goodness-of-fit of the model using mid-pseudo-residuals

Furthermore, normality tests can be carried out on these pseudo-residuals. For example, Jarque-Bera normality tests do not reject the null of a standard Gaussian for the mid-pseudo residuals at the 10% confidence level.

We will be able to compare this fit to those obtained on real world default data in the next sections.

One can also use parametric bootstrap to obtain the standard deviation as well as the variance-covariance matrix of the estimated parameters. Parametric bootstrap is described in Annex 7.1.3. It generates 100 time-series of default from the fitted model, fits a HMM model to each of the scenario using the same starting guess than for fitting the model for the first time, and 100 iterations for the maximisation of the log-likelihood in each of the fit, and allows to obtain statistics on the fitted parameters. We obtain the following correlation matrix:

	p_1	p_2	a_{11}	a_{22}
p_1	1	0.5431	0.3562	-0.1164
p_2		1	0.1571	-0.2162
a_{11}			1	0.4693
a_{22}				1

as well as the mean and standard deviation of each parameter, which are reported in the table below:

	true generating model	mean est.	standard deviation
p_1	0.0038	0.0039	0.0005
p_2	0.0076	0.0079	0.0009
a_{11}	0.7780	0.8668	0.0876
a_{22}	0.836	0.8535	0.1221

Figure 7.3 below indicate the histograms of the empirical distribution of each fitted parameter p_1, p_2, a_{11} and a_{22}. As can be seen from the top two histograms, p_1 and p_2 can reasonably be assumed normally distributed. From this we deduce the 95% confidence interval as 1.96 times the standard deviation: $p_1 = 0.0039 \pm 0.00098$ and $p_2 = 0.0079 \pm 0.001764$. As the upper bound for p_1 (0.00488) is lower than the lower bound for p_2 (0.006136), we can safely say that the two distinct states are well identified (at a 95% confidence level).

7.1. EFFICIENT ALGORITHMS

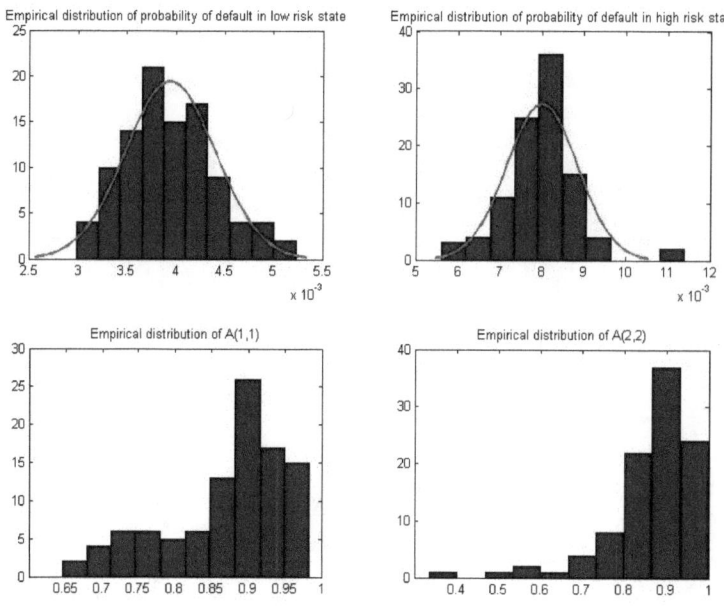

Figure 7.3: Empirical estimates dispersion

www.ingramcontent.com/pod-product-compliance
Lightning Source LLC
Chambersburg PA
CBHW080718190526
45169CB00006B/2427